GOOD HOUSEKEEPING
MICROWAVE
HANDBOOK

GOOD HOUSEKEEPING
MICROWAVE HANDBOOK

Margaret Weale

EBURY PRESS
LONDON

Published by Ebury Press
National Magazine House
72 Broadwick Street
London W1V 2BP

Reprinted 1982

ISBN 0 85223 230 6 (paperback)
ISBN 0 85223 222 5 (hardback)

Written by Margaret Weale
Designed by Derek Morrison
Illustrated by Ivan Ripley
Photographs by Melvin Grey
Cover photograph by Bill Richmond

Ebury Press would like to thank TI Creda Limited for the loan of
their Creda Mealmaster microwave cooker for use in the
photograph on the front cover. The recipes within the book were
tested in several different microwave cookers from a variety
of manufacturers.

Filmset by Advanced Filmsetters (Glasgow) Ltd
Printed and bound by Cambridge University Press

CONTENTS

CONTENTS *(contd)*

Recipes

GOLDEN RULES

Whatever make of microwave oven you have, these general rules apply. For more detailed information about the various methods and techniques of microwave cooking turn to the appropriate section in the following pages.

1 Read the manufacturer's instruction book carefully as microwave ovens vary from model to model.
2 Never use metal or melamine containers.
3 Choose straight-sided, round rather than square, dishes, to give the maximum exposure to the microwaves.
4 If in doubt undercook. A few seconds too long can spoil a dish and you can always put the dish back in the oven if it isn't quite done.
5 Remember that food will go on cooking for 5–10 minutes when it is taken out of the oven. So always allow for 'standing time'.
6 Cover food to keep it moist. Use pierced cling or microwave film, or a non-metallic lid.
7 Arrange food carefully to ensure even cooking. A general rule is the thinnest part towards the centre and place items like buns or potatoes in a circle rather than a row.
8 Cut vegetables into even-sized pieces.
9 Stir foods at least once during the cooking time unless your oven has a turntable.
10 When using boiling or roasting bags, prick them to prevent bursting.
11 Always prick whole potatoes, tomatoes and fruit to prevent bursting.
12 When doubling a recipe, allow one-third to one-half extra cooking time. When halving the amount only two-thirds to three-quarters of the original cooking time will be needed.
13 Never attempt to defrost food in a closed container or bag. Remove lids or covers, pierce bags, remove metal ties and replace them with string.
14 Have your oven professionally checked once a year.
15 Reheat baked goods and pastry on a microwave roasting rack so that air can circulate underneath.
16 Never attempt to deep fat fry in a microwave oven.
17 Beware of hot centres. Remember that microwaved foods reach a higher temperature and so cook more quickly where there is a concentration of fat or sugar, so take care when biting into foods such as jam doughnuts or sausage rolls.
18 Always leave a cup of water in the microwave oven when it is not in use.

MICROWAVE FACTS

The microwave oven is the most significant innovation in cooking technology since the home freezer, and will probably become an equally standard feature in our kitchens. It has been called 'the greatest cooking discovery since fire'; this may seem an exaggerated claim, but it does help to emphasise the most important point about microwave ovens: that they really do represent a totally new concept in cooking. Microwave cooking is a brand new technique which needs to be understood to be successful; but once the mysteries are made clear there is nothing difficult about it nor need there be any concern about safety.

Why Have a Microwave Oven?

Microwave ovens are no longer the playthings of rich gadget lovers. Their design has been improved to meet people's *needs* and now they really can make life easier. They are particularly useful for families whose pattern of life demands quick meals at varying times, for example, when both husband and wife are out at work, when a member of the household works irregular hours or shifts, or when an erratic teenage family needs to be fed at the times suited to their busy programmes. Anyone living alone would find one ideal for cooking individual meals as it doesn't waste any energy cooking small portions like conventional ovens do, and its simple controls make it perfect for the elderly or disabled.

A microwave oven won't replace a conventional cooker, but used together the two will complement each other in any number of ways, helping the cook to extend his or her kitchen repertoire.

The Advantages of a Microwave Oven

Look at the basic advantages listed here, learn to use your microwave oven and you'll discover many more.

Speed

As a rough guide, microwave cooking takes about one third to one quarter of the conventional cooking time. This varies according to the density of the food, starting temperature (straight from the fridge or at room temperature, for example) and the amount. You can cook a whole chicken in half an hour or a jacket potato in 4 minutes.

Economy

Energy is only consumed during the actual cooking time. There is no need to preheat the oven since heat is generated instantly within the food as soon as the oven is switched on. It switches off automatically at the end of the pre-set cooking period and even if you open the door to look at the food while it is cooking no heat is wasted as the power switches off at once—until the door is closed again.

Cool Kitchens

As the oven itself never gets hot, the kitchen will be cooler. Cooking smells and steam are minimal. This characteristic is obviously an advantage if you want to position the cooker in an eating area rather than in the kitchen.

Cleanliness

A microwave oven is much easier to clean than an ordinary one, as the interior walls remain cool during cooking. Spills and splashes do not bake on to the sides, base and top. All that is needed is a quick wipe round with a damp cloth.

Less Washing up

If you choose the right kind of dish or plate (see page 34) food can be cooked and served in the same container. Dishes don't get hot in the oven so it is easy to bring the food straight to the table without dishing it up first. If you want a quick cup of coffee, you can make it in a mug to save a saucepan and you can cook vegetables in their serving dish and heat rolls in a basket.

Flavour

Foods cook in their own juices, retaining all their natural flavours. As they are cooked so quickly, using the minimum amount of water, vitamins and nutrients are also preserved. Many foods can be cooked without butter or additional fat—an added bonus for weight watchers or those trying to avoid too much cholesterol in their diet.

Defrosting

Use the oven for thawing frozen food in a fraction of the time it normally takes, following the manufacturer's instructions. This will mean either using the defrost button or turning the oven on and off at frequent intervals (see page 1). Defrosting too fast can result in the outside of the food starting to cook before the centre has thawed. A loaf of sliced bread, beefburgers, or a prepared frozen meal for one, only need about 3–4 minutes in the oven.

Reheating

To be able to reheat food without spoiling its appearance or flavour is an advantage in any household. About $1\frac{1}{2}$–2 minutes in the oven is sufficient to reheat a helping of food set aside for a latecomer. It will come out looking as if it has been freshly cooked.

Versatility

Most people think of microwave ovens only in terms of cooking meals quickly, but that's not the whole story. It's worth knowing that it can also speed the preparation of meals by softening butter and margarine, melting chocolate, dissolving jelly cubes, roasting nuts and much, much more.

Mobility

Microwave ovens do not require any special installation other than needing a stable surface. Plug your oven into any 13 or 15 amp socket outlet. Use it in the dining or breakfast room if that's convenient. Better still, because it is heavy, keep it on a trolley and trundle it where it is needed, even on to the patio for outdoor meals.

Ease of Use

Because microwave ovens can be positioned at counter height and most dishes are cool enough to be removed without an oven glove, they are often preferred by the blind, those in wheelchairs and other disabled people who find them simpler and safer to use. Children find microwave ovens easy to use too.

How the Microwave Oven Works

Nowadays much household equipment involves advanced technology; people accept video-recorders, hi-fis, freezers and dishwashers with mini-computer programmes without a second thought. Why then are so many people sceptical about microwave ovens? These 'space-age' cookers still seem to have an air of mystery surrounding them, yet the same shortwave energy which powers them is used in television sets, sunlamps and much common medical equipment. Microwave ovens have been in commercial use for many years; it is only recently however that models for use in the home have become generally available. Maybe this is why people have begun to wonder how they work, and have come up with some weird and wonderful answers which are far from the truth! But the basic principles of microwave cooking are simple: once you've understood them, it will be easy to learn how to apply them to your everyday cooking requirements.

What are Microwaves?

Many people think of electrical energy only being transmitted through wires, but it can also be transmitted through space by electro-magnetic waves. Microwaves are in fact electro-magnetic waves, converted from electrical energy. They are of very short length and high frequency, and fall into the part of the electro-magnetic spectrum occupied by television and FM (short wave) broadcasting. They are also present in ordinary daylight, the warmth of the sun, ordinary light bulbs and fluorescent lights. The waves, which travel in straight lines, are of a single length, very short—less than 12.5 cm (5 inches)—hence the term *microwave*.

How Microwaves are Produced in a Cooker

When the microwave oven is plugged in (to a 13 or 15 amp socket—no special wiring is required) the electricity is converted to microwaves by a tube called a magnetron. The waves are then channelled into the interior of the oven, usually from the top, by a waveguide and stirrer. This stirrer, which is similar to a fan blade and is driven by the fan motor, distributes the microwaves evenly to different parts of the oven cavity. (Some models have a turntable on which to place the food instead, which has the same effect.)

The magnetron will *only* produce microwaves when the timer is set, the oven door closed, and the power switched on, and then only for the duration of the pre-set time. As soon as the timer switches off, or if the oven door is opened during the cooking period, the magnetron automatically turns itself off, immediately stops producing microwaves, and so cooking by microwave energy stops instantly.

How do Microwaves Cook Food?

Microwaves, like any electro-magnetic waves, including light rays, have three important characteristics. That is, they can either be reflected, transmitted or absorbed by things with which they come into contact.

Microwaves cannot penetrate metal and are reflected by it, just as a mirror reflects light. Thus the basic principle of a microwave oven is to trap microwaves which are then absorbed by the food placed inside it. The waves bounce off the metal sides, roof and base of the oven interior, as well as off the metal mesh screen on the oven door.

Although microwaves can't penetrate metal, there are many other substances which they can pass straight through (transmit) without producing heat, just as light passes through a window. Such substances are pottery and china, glass, glass ceramic, paper, wood and some plastics. Where there is a shelf or turntable on which food is placed inside the oven, it is usually made of a ceramic material. It is raised off the metal base of the oven to allow the microwaves to bounce off the base and cook the underside of the food.

1 In a microwave cooker, the magnetron converts electrical energy to microwaves. These are reflected by the metal walls of the oven, but pass straight through non-metallic cooking containers.

2 Microwaves are attracted to food but can only penetrate to a depth of 5 cm (2 inches). The heat generated in this outer layer cooks food at the centre by conduction.

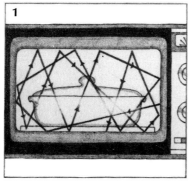

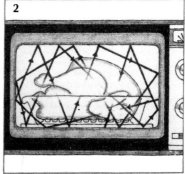

Microwaves are absorbed by water, and since all foods contain a certain amount of water, they readily absorb microwave energy. The microwave oven interior is designed to direct the microwaves produced in it on to food placed inside it, and the door seal prevents any from escaping. The microwaves penetrate the food by about 5 cm (2 inches) and are attracted to the tiny water molecules in the food. This causes them to vibrate at an incredibly high speed—2,450 million times a second (otherwise known as having a frequency of 2,450 MHz). (Microwaves are also attracted to the sugar and fat content in food, and have the same effect on them.) As the vibrating molecules rub against each other this creates friction, which in turn produces heat within the food—just like rubbing your hands together. The heat-producing activity spreads from the initial point of penetration which is why you can cook foods more than 5 cm (2 inches) thick. As a result, microwave ovens do not need preheating like conventional ovens as the microwave energy produces heat inside the food molecules as soon as they are generated by the magnetron.

You can see from this that the way heat is generated in microwave cooking is fundamentally different from conventional ovens, hobs and grills. Microwaves aren't in themselves hot, they only produce heat within the food. Microwaves travel directly through the air and the cooking container to the food, which is why both the inside of the oven cavity and the container remain cool during the cooking (though a container may sometimes be warmed subsequently by the heat from the food cooked in or on it). As soon as the magnetron stops producing microwaves they disperse into the atmosphere—no residual microwave energy stays in the food.

Microwave cooking is a moist form of cookery, so you may find that moisture collects on the inside of the oven during use. This is quite normal, and occurs when the steam from food condenses on the cool interior walls and door. The oven vent will release most of the steam, but even so, you may on occasions notice slight condensation or feel warm air around the door when using the oven. This is also quite usual on some models, for although the door seal is designed to prevent microwave energy escaping, it does not necessarily have to be airtight.

Are They Safe?

The microwave oven is one of the safest kitchen appliances—it has no sharp edges or moving parts on which to cut yourself, and its unique form of heat generation within the food helps prevent accidental burns and scalding. Even so questions are often asked about the safety of microwave cooking itself, usually because people do not know or are confused about how microwave cookers work.

Most of the confusion arises from the fact that microwaves are a form of radiation. But the word radiation is often misused. It simply refers to the passage of electro-magnetic energy through space. There are two types of radiation; the safe, non-ionising type to which microwaves belong, and the ionising type which can be hazardous, like X-rays, gamma rays and ultra-violet rays.

Non-ionising rays like microwaves do not cause a breakdown of cells nor a chemical change in the organism exposed to them. In other words low level exposure to microwave energy, such as from a microwave cooker in normal use, is not harmful to humans. Nevertheless, people are concerned about the possibility of leakage from a microwave oven or cooker, and they need to be reassured.

British Standard Specifications for Microwave Ovens

Manufacturers have gone to great lengths to ensure that the microwaves stay *inside* the oven. All domestic microwave ovens sold in Britain and bearing the BEAB (British Electrotechnical Approvals Board) label are made to comply with British Standard 3456 (BS 3456: Part 2: Section 2.33: 1976 'Microwave ovens'). To ensure that this British Standard is maintained, models are independently tested at the Electricity Council Appliance Testing Laboratories for both electrical safety and microwave leakage. There are strict maximum limits on leakage, which must not exceed 5 milliwatts per square centimetre at a distance of 5 centimetres from the oven door throughout the 'life' of the cooker. In practice, leakage levels are much lower than this. In addition it's important to realise that the radiation spreads out if it escapes, so that the amount of radiation decreases rapidly the further away it travels from its sources. This means that even if the maximum allowed leakage of 5 milliwatts per square centimetre was measured at a distance of 5 centimetres from the oven door, this would have decreased to as little as 0.005 milliwatts at an arm's length from the oven door. (And a milliwatt is anyway a minute amount of microwave energy!)

How Microwave Ovens are Tested

The following points help illustrate the careful testing applied to microwave oven doors:

1 The door is opened and closed 100,000 times, and measurements are taken after every 10,000 operations.
2 The interlocks on the door are also tested 100,000 times, and these too are checked after every 10,000 operations.
3 Extra special attention is given to ensure that even if only one of the interlocks failed, microwave energy could not be switched on.

These 100,000 operations are equivalent to using a microwave oven seven times a day, seven days a week, fifty-two weeks a year for almost forty years!

Remember too that there is no possible way that microwaves can be present when the oven door is opened, because as soon as the door catch is moved a fraction, the microwaves stop being generated—just like switching a light off. All ovens must have two primary interlocks to prevent the unit from operating when the door is open, plus another interlock which monitors the two primary interlocks. The endurance tests also simulate years of wear on door seals.

Checking Leakage Levels

Qualified microwave oven service engineers use a special meter which registers the level of emission when the oven is in use. Microwave ovens are tested individually when they leave the factory, and a meter check—which can be done in your home and takes just a few minutes—should be part of a regular annual servicing.

If you want to have your microwave oven checked in this way, you should contact your dealer, manufacturer, or appointed service agent. Some local council Environmental Health Departments also have this testing equipment, and are prepared to test the oven in your home.

Further Reassurances

1 Like all other appliances, microwave ovens must comply with the requirements of the safety regulations of the Consumer Safety Act 1978, as well as the Health and Safety at Work Act 1974.
2 The Department of Prices and Consumer Protection considers that microwave ovens built to satisfy British Standards are safe, and they have issued statements to this effect.
3 The National Radiological Protection Board also considers that microwave ovens which satisfy British Standards requirements are safe, and they too have issued statements to this effect.
4 There is no proven evidence anywhere in the world of any user of a microwave oven being harmed.

Heart Pacemakers

Certain types of cardiac pacemakers may be affected by microwaves. There are basically two types of cardiac pacemakers: 'fixed', which constantly stimulate the heart, and 'demand' which operate only when they sense that the heart is weakening. It is the few early unshielded models of this latter 'demand' type pacemaker which are susceptible to interference from electromagnetic fields, caused for example by some car motors, electric razors and, in this case, microwave ovens. Newer pacemakers are shielded against this interference and interruption, but if there is any doubt, be sure to get medical advice and warn any visitors to your home who may be fitted with a pacemaker to stay out of the room when the oven is in use.

A Last Word on Safety

Food is cooked by heat whether it is cooked conventionally or by microwave energy, and the only difference is the type of heat penetration. Microwaves do not make food radioactive. Food cooked in a microwave oven is not harmful to eat, even only a second after it has been removed from the oven.

Choosing a Microwave Oven

At present, there are three main types of microwave oven on the market; countertop portable microwave ovens, double oven microwave cookers and combination ovens. Whichever type of microwave oven you are interested in, the cost varies greatly from model to model, and the price will obviously influence your decision. But it is important to choose the model or type specially designed for the job you want it to do. Consider the features of each type and model as they would fit into your lifestyle, and be sure to anticipate any future changes which are likely to happen to you during the next few months or years, such as the size of your household, their age and their work schedule.

Think also about the type of cooking you and your family prefer, and also consider where you will be positioning your cooker in the kitchen in relation to existing appliances, taking into account its dimensions and ventilation requirements. Ask yourself a few preliminary questions, too. Does the oven carry the BEAB mark of safety label or the Electricity Council's 'approved for safety' label? Does it carry a guarantee? Is there a full or limited warranty? Is there a longer guarantee period for the magnetron, and if so for how long? How comprehensive is the use and care manual supplied with the oven and what are the servicing arrangements? In addition, look at the various features listed in the next few pages and compare them and the warranty arrangements between similar models. For example, look inside the oven. Does it have an easy to clean surface? Is there a splatter guard or cover over the stirrer blades. Is the cavity large enough for your needs? Does it have indicator lights, a defrost switch if you own a freezer? This will help you make a sensible choice for an appliance which should be a valuable addition to your kitchen for quite some time to come.

Countertop Portable Microwave Ovens

These are the most popular type of microwave oven in Britain today. Countertop microwave ovens are nominally portable, but they are rather heavy to be carried from room to room with any frequency. However some manufacturers offer a sturdy trolley as an optional extra, for this very purpose. The oven fits neatly on the top shelf and there is usually a lower shelf or cupboard below for carrying dishes or other utensils. Other models can be 'built in' to kitchen or dining room units. It is best to consult the individual manufacturers and follow their recommendations if you want to do this with your oven. Otherwise, countertop models are ideal for placing on a convenient worktop in your kitchen.

Two-Level Microwave Cookers

This type of microwave oven is relatively new in Britain. The microwave energy is usually fed into the sides rather than the top of the oven cavity. There is a rack or shelf in the oven, sometimes with a choice of two runner positions, on which food can be placed as well as on the floor of the oven to provide simultaneous two-level cooking facilities. Normally the food on the rack receives more microwave energy than the food on the floor of the oven, so foods which require a longer cooking period can go on top, while those which need less—or perhaps only need heating or re-heating—can be placed underneath. For even cooking results, make sure that dishes are not placed directly one above the other. When only one food is being cooked at a time, the rack is removed and the food is placed on the floor of the oven. To use this type of cooker efficiently requires a certain amount of planning but can be useful for a large family.

Double Oven Microwave Cookers

These are available in two forms: either as a free standing cooker with a hob, a microwave oven at eye-level and a conventional oven under the hob; or as a built-in double oven unit, housing a microwave oven and separate conventional oven, leaving you the choice of a separate hob to be built in where you want it. A grill is usually incorporated in the top of the conventional oven. These appliances offer the advantages of complementary cooking in one unit. For example, you can start cooking a double crust apple pie in the microwave oven and then transfer it to the conventional oven to brown and crisp the pastry. Complementary cooking can also be employed to improve the appearance and flavour of casseroles and stews which use the cheaper cuts of meat. The meat can first be browned on the conventional cooker hob before cooking in the microwave oven. The upper microwave ovens of these double oven cookers will of course perform in the same way as a countertop portable microwave oven.

The ordinary countertop microwave oven can be used to complement a conventional cooker in exactly the same way, so a double oven microwave cooker would probably only be worth considering if your conventional cooker needs replacing at the time you are considering buying a microwave oven.

First course: from the top left, clockwise, Cream of Mushroom Soup (page 75), Kipper Pâté (page 77), and Soused Herrings (page 86).

Combination Ovens

These are appliances offering both microwave and conventional cooking facilities in the same oven, but they are not yet readily available in Britain. Some manufacturers offer countertop combination ovens, others incorporate the oven in a free standing cooker with a hob. There is usually a grill in the top of the oven.

Microwave and conventional oven cooking can be used together, separately, or in sequence, as preferred. With the oven door closed, it is sometimes also possible to grill and cook by microwave energy at the same time. Conventional baking or cooking, teamed with microwave speed enables you to cook an entire meal at once, but in about half the normal time. The microwave energy output in this type of combination oven is usually lower than the output of ovens designed purely to produce microwave energy such as countertop microwave ovens or the separate microwave ovens of double oven cookers. This type of oven, would be ideal for families who enjoy traditional cooking and baking, but who also want to benefit from the convenience and speed of microwave cooking.

Standard Features

You could be forgiven for thinking that you need to complete a computer programming course before operating some microwave ovens. In fact, though they may vary on different models—some are featured separately and others are combined—they are simple to understand and use. Once you are used to them, you will find the basic principles are the same on most models and the more versatile the controls, the more convenient they are. The features discussed below are those available on most countertop ovens, but most of them will also be found on double and two level microwave cookers.

On/Off Control

This control is sometimes called a POWER ON button. As well as switching the oven ON and OFF, it may also start the cooling fan and switch on the oven interior light, but it does not usually control the generation of microwave energy.

Cook or Start Control

This control switches on the microwave energy for cooking, heating and defrosting food, but cannot be operated until the oven door is closed. When the oven door is opened, the microwave energy is automatically switched off. To resume cooking, the door must be closed and this control switched on again.

Timer

The timer controls the cooking period and may be either the mechanical or digital type. It is set to the required number of

Breakfast: from the top left, clockwise, hot Bread Rolls and Croissants (page 47), Coffee (page 67), Scrambled Eggs (page 79) with rolled Bacon Slices (page 91).

minutes and/or seconds, and when the time has elapsed a bell or buzzer usually sounds to indicate that cooking has stopped and the oven has switched off automatically.

Oven Door

Most models have side opening doors, although some are available with drop down or slide up doors which are operated by a latch or button. There is usually a transparent mesh panel in the door through which you can watch food cooking provided of course that the oven has an interior light. All microwave ovens incorporate a safety mechanism which ensures that they cannot be operated until the door is securely closed. When closed, the oven door provides an effective seal against microwave leakage when the oven is in use.

Oven Cavity

This is the cooking space. It is a smooth, metal-lined box, which may have a plastic coating. Food is cooked on the oven floor and it is worth checking different models carefully to check they are easy to clean. Some models have removable glass floors or shelves, others have built in ceramic shelves and many have removable turntables. All of these have been specially designed and positioned to allow microwaves to penetrate the food placed on them from all angles, including the base. There is usually an interior light which comes on when the oven is switched on. Some models accommodate a microwave 'stirrer', behind a splatter guard or cover in the roof of the cavity.

Oven Vent and Filter

All ovens have some type of vent, either in the form of a grid or small holes, positioned at the back or on the sides, front or top of the oven. The purpose of the vent is to allow a proportion of moisture to escape from the oven during cooking. Some models have air filters, through which cooling air passes into the oven space. It doesn't cool the food inside the cooker, only the internal components. The filter is removable and should be checked and cleaned periodically according to the manufacturer's instructions to ensure that it is kept free from grease and dust.

Oven Power Output

The power output of a microwave oven is the amount of microwave energy available within the oven cavity for cooking, heating and defrosting food. Remember that although the input to an oven might be quoted as 1,000 watts, the quoted output into the oven cavity could be only 500 watts—in other words the 'cooking power' of the oven is 500 watts. The remaining watts have been used by the magnetron to convert electricity into microwaves. Most domestic countertop microwave ovens have output wattages within the 500W to 700W range. These wattages are usually displayed on the rating plate of the oven, and the power output is normally referred to in the Instruction Manual.

The higher the oven output, the faster the rate of cooking. When the power is doubled, the cooking rate is also doubled— and the cooking time halved. However, bearing in mind the speed of cooking by microwave energy, the difference in time taken to cook food in an oven of lower output compared with an oven of higher output might only be a matter of seconds rather than minutes.

Additional Features of Microwave Ovens

Many additional features have been added to the basic counter-top portable oven, and although they may add to the initial cost they are well worth considering before you buy.

Rotating Platform/Turntable

All microwave ovens, even the most expensive ones, are likely to have hot and cold spots. To ensure even cooking, food must occasionally be turned during cooking, heating or defrosting. As an alternative to doing this manually, some microwave ovens have a turntable or rotating platform which automatically rotates the food through the microwave patterns within the oven. When a turntable is used, the need to stir or turn food or turn dishes during cooking is reduced to a minimum.

Rotating platforms or turntables are made of toughened glass or glass ceramic and can be removed for cleaning. Some models of oven must not be used without the turntable in position, whereas the turntable can be removed from other models and replaced by a suitable dish or container to accommodate larger items of food. In this case, it is advisable to turn the dish or container by hand instead during the heating or cooking period. In any case, always follow individual manufacturer's recommendations as to whether or not the oven can be operated without the turntable in position.

Defrost Control

Automatic defrosting is a major development and provides even defrosting of frozen food. It is extremely useful and is now incorporated in many microwave ovens. When this control is used in conjunction with the timer, the microwave energy into the oven is automatically cycled on and off to allow rest periods in between short bursts of microwave energy. In ovens without a defrost control this has to be done by hand. The defrost control can sometimes also be used for foods which are better cooked more slowly, such as a casserole.

Variable Power

This offers even greater flexibility, allowing you to select the speed at which food cooks. Like the defrost control, this variable power control allows the power level to be altered, automatically controlling the rate of heating or cooking. The number of settings on the control varies between models. They may be described as High, Medium, Low or graduated in numbers or expressed as familiar cooking methods such as Roast, Simmer, Bake, Reheat, Defrost. The control also provides a Full Power or High setting for the normal quick cooking of most foods.

Indicator Lights

These are a useful reminder that a cooking operation has been set, is in progress, or has been completed.

Cooking Guide

This is usually in the form of a panel on the front or top of the oven and gives basic information for different cooking operations.

Browning Element/ Integral Grill

Some microwave ovens incorporate an element towards the top of the oven for the purpose of browning food before or after microwave cooking, but this is not a common feature. If you already have a perfectly good grill on your conventional oven there is really no need to buy a microwave oven which supplies you with another.

Browning Dish

Some manufacturers provide a special dish or plate to brown smaller items of food which are normally grilled or fried, such as sausages, beefburgers, steaks, chops, bacon or eggs. These would normally cook too quickly in a microwave oven to allow them to brown. The browning dish or plate is made of a special material which absorbs microwave energy. It is heated empty in the microwave oven for a predetermined time. The food is then placed on the hot surface and is immediately seared and browned. During the subsequent microwave cooking, the food is turned over to brown the other side. The dish comes complete with a toughened glass lid, and the flat plate has a channel around the outside to collect excess fat or juices from the food being cooked.

Temperature Probe/Food Sensor

The temperature probe enables you to control microwave cooking by the internal temperature of the food, rather than by time, and is particularly useful when cooking joints of meat or when reheating food. The probe has a flexible connection to a socket inside the oven. The point is inserted into the thickest part of the food being cooked and the desired temperature selected, rather than setting the timer. When the internal temperature reaches the pre-set amount, the oven either switches itself off or reduces to a lower power setting to keep the food warm until needed. It takes a lot of guesswork out of microwave cookery of large, dense items, as you must not use a conventional meat thermometer inside a microwave oven. However a temperature probe can only be used at best as a guide to the readiness of food as it only tests the temperature in one place. It is advisable to test by other conventional methods as well.

Touch Controls

These are built in to the outer front panel of some models, and are operated simply by touching the relevant space with the fingertips. They have exactly the same function as more conventional controls.

Memory Controls

These are a recent additional feature to be added to a few of the more expensive models, most of which are imported from America. They enable the cook to programme two power settings, so, for example, cooking can be automatically slowed down after the initial high power setting has brought food to the boil. Whilst these controls perhaps bring greater convenience and flexibility they also tend to take some of the simplicity out of microwave cookery.

Installation

Countertop microwave ovens can look misleadingly small in the showroom. Check the external dimensions of the oven and note the position of the vents—if they're at the back you can't push the oven against a wall; if at the top it mustn't be squeezed under a cupboard or shelf. The physical installation of the oven is relatively simple, all it requires is a firm support on which to stand, a correctly fused 13 amp or 15 amp three pin plug and a convenient, fused socket outlet. It can be placed on a worktop, table, on a trolley or perhaps as part of a built-in scheme. Other types of oven may *need* to be built in, but in any case, remember to consult individual manufacturer's instructions and recommendations.

Checking the Oven

If you have the simple type, check the oven carefully when you get it home. Remove all packaging, instruction books and any other materials from the oven interior. Inspect the oven carefully for any damage such as a misaligned door, bent hinges, bent broken or loose latches, damaged seal around the door, dents or holes in the door screen, or dents in the oven exterior or interior. If there is any damage whatsoever, do not attempt to repair or operate the unit. Instead, contact your dealer—or manufacturer's nearest service depot—who will arrange for the oven to be inspected by qualified service personnel. If the oven appears satisfactory, proceed to install it according to the manufacturer's instructions, following the specific recommendations precisely, and noting any special ventilation requirements. Don't forget to complete the Registration or Guarantee Card and return it to the manufacturer.

Oven Care

It's difficult to resist trying out any new appliance as soon as you get it home, but with a microwave oven especially it's worth exercising a little patience. There are certain rules which you have to learn to get the best out of your new oven. Some may seem obvious to you, but it is surprising what mistakes people have made in the past.

1 Always read the manufacturer's instruction manual, and be sure to follow the correct electrical specifications for your oven.
2 Do not remove the outer case or oven door at any time.
3 Never close the oven door with anything between it and the oven face, or the door seal could be broken. Do not dry or hang tea towels on the door.
4 Never line the oven with foil, paper or any material of any kind as this could cause damage.
5 Never attempt to insert objects through the mesh panel.
6 Never tamper with oven safety switches or built-in interlocks.
7 Do not lean heavily on the oven door.
8 Never operate the oven without food inside, since this can damage the magnetron and may also invalidate the guarantee.
9 Keep a china cup or glass of water in the oven when it is not being used for cooking. If the oven is accidentally switched on the microwave energy will be channelled into the water, so preventing damage to the magnetron.
10 Do not use the oven for storing utensils, books or papers.
11 Always ask for qualified help if the oven does not appear to be operating satisfactorily. Do not try to repair the oven yourself.
12 Have the oven checked or serviced every twelve months, or as recommended by the manufacturer.

Oven Cleaning

As the interior walls of the oven aren't directly heated, the inside of the oven remains relatively cool in use. This means that splashing and spillage do not burn on to the oven's interior surfaces as they do in a conventional oven, and so the microwave oven is very easy to clean. However, it is still important to clean the oven interior each time it is used as any spillage on the oven interior will absorb microwave energy and slow down the cooking next time you use the oven. As with any electric appliance, it is advisable to disconnect the oven from the electricity supply, during cleaning.

Cleaning the Interior

1 Wipe over the entire oven interior and inside of the door with a damp cloth after each use. Unless the manufacturer specifically recommends proprietary cleaners, these should not be used. When cooking various foods one after the other, wipe any excess moisture from the inside of the oven, including the door and the door seal, in between each dish.

2 Removable bases, glass shelves and turntables should also be cleaned. If they are broken, they should not be replaced by anything other than a replacement supplied by the manufacturer.

3 Never use aerosol cleaners, caustic cleaners or harsh abrasives, and never use a knife or other utensil to try to remove a stubborn mark, since these can not only spoil the appearance and make subsequent cleaning more difficult, but can also damage the surfaces. If the walls of the oven are scratched this may distort the wave pattern and could lead to the production of small sparks (known as arcing), which in turn could damage the magnetron.

4 If any dirty mark proves difficult to remove, heat a fairly large bowl of water in the oven until it is steaming hot. The vapour should help to loosen the dirt which can then be removed easily with a damp cloth. Use a cloth rinsed in warm soapy water to remove grease, rinsing afterwards with clear water, and finally polishing with a soft dry cloth.

5 Do not allow grease or food particles to build up on or around the door seal. In order to maintain a good seal it is important that this is kept absolutely clean by wiping with soapy water, rinsing with clear water and drying thoroughly. If there is any sign that the seal has been damaged or has become dislodged, do not use the oven again until it has been repaired or replaced.

6 If your oven incorporates an air filter or a splatter guard covering the stirrer in the roof of the oven interior, both of these must be kept clean according to the manufacturer's instructions. If the filter becomes blocked, the cooling mechanism will no longer be effective, resulting in possible damage to the oven.

7 To remove smells from the inside of the oven, place a cup or bowl containing 3 parts water and 1 part lemon juice in the cavity and boil for 5–10 minutes. Wipe and dry the oven.

Cleaning the Exterior

1 The outside of the oven should be wiped over with a damp cloth or according to the manufacturer's special instructions.

2 Do not splash water over the exterior vents. These should be wiped over occasionally to remove any condensation.

COOKING THEORY

A completely new cooking concept needs to be properly explained, even when it is as easy as cooking by microwaves, so these next few pages are designed to help you understand the special cooking techniques, the different properties of food which influence microwave cooking and the types of utensils you can use in your microwave oven.

Factors which Affect Microwave Cooking Times

Whether the food is to be defrosted, reheated or cooked from its raw state, success depends on correct timing and correct power level setting on ovens with variable controls. The amount of time required is always very short, but even a few seconds can mean the difference between success and failure. Timing will be affected by certain factors, such as the type of food, the recipe method, the quantity and so on.

Starting Temperature of Food

The colder the food, the longer it will take to heat. In other words food taken from the refrigerator will take longer to heat or cook than food at room temperature. Similarly, refrigerated foods will heat or cook more quickly than frozen foods. Remember too that room temperatures vary depending on the time of the year, so cooking times may need to be extended slightly on cold winter days.

Composition of Food

Microwaves are attracted to the water, fat and sugar molecules in food. Water is drawn to the surface of the food during cooking before it evaporates, preventing foods like bread and cakes from browning or forming a crust. During the longer cooking times required to cook turkeys or large joints of meat, the natural fats which are drawn to the surface are allowed enough time to brown. Smaller joints or portions of meat and poultry also contain fat, but the short microwave cooking time is not long enough for them to brown. Foods with a high fat and sugar content will heat much more quickly than foods with a low fat and sugar content. For example the jam in the centre of a jam doughnut will reach a higher temperature than the surrounding plainer dough, and the fat on a slice of meat will heat more quickly than the leaner meat on the same slice. Meat which is marbled with fat will cook more evenly than meat with larger fatty areas and very lean areas, because microwaves are attracted primarily to the fat rather than the leaner meat areas. Since bones conduct heat, meat on the bone will cook more quickly than boned, but the latter will cook more evenly.

Sensitive Foods Some foods can easily be overcooked in a microwave oven because of their very high water, sugar or fat content. These foods include cheese, eggs, cream, soured cream, baked beans, kidney beans, mushrooms, scallops, snails, oysters and mayonnaise. If overcooked they will toughen, curdle or 'pop'; for this reason they should always be cooked for the minimum time recommended and watched carefully during the cooking period. In ovens with 'variable power', these foods are normally cooked at lower power levels, to allow them to cook more gently.

N.B. Do not cook eggs in their shells. Microwave cooking is so fast that enormous pressure builds up inside the shell which may cause the egg to explode.

Quantity of Food

Small amounts of food require less time to cook than larger quantities of the same food. This is because they receive more concentrated amounts of microwave energy. As a general guide, if you double the amount of food to be cooked, you should increase the cooking time by between about one third and one half—and check for readiness at the shortest calculated time. Similarly, when cooking quantities are halved, the cooking time should be decreased to slightly more than half the time allowed for the original full quantity of that food. It is essential always to underestimate rather than overestimate cooking time in a microwave oven. Food which is undercooked can always be returned to the oven for further cooking, but there is absolutely no remedy for overcooked spoilt food.

Density of Food

A dense food such as meat will take longer to defrost, reheat or cook than porous, light and airy foods such as bread, cakes and puddings. Microwaves cannot penetrate as deeply into denser, heavier foods, so the centre is heated and cooked by the conduction of heat from the hotter outer surfaces. A joint of meat may look cooked on the outside, while it is still underdone in the centre. This is fine, if you want a rare joint of beef, but meat which has to be fully cooked, like pork and poultry, may have to stand after cooking to allow heat to be transferred to the centre without overcooking the outside. Minced meat is less dense than a piece of steak, so a beefburger will heat more quickly than a steak. Cakes, puddings and bread, on the other hand, are rapidly penetrated by microwaves because of their porous texture, and extreme care must be taken to prevent overheating these foods. A typical example which illustrates this rapid penetration of porous food is the fact that a 450-g (1-lb) Christmas pudding can be reheated in a microwave oven in just over two minutes!

Size and Shape of Food

The size and shape of the food must also be taken into consideration. Several small pieces of food will cook faster than single larger pieces of the same food. For example, pieces of meat cut into small cubes for stews and casseroles will cook more quickly than the same quantity of meat cooked as a joint. This is because the microwaves which penetrate the food to a depth of between 2–4 cm ($\frac{3}{4}$–$1\frac{1}{2}$ inches) will cook the smaller cubes quickly from all sides, but the larger joint of meat will rely on heat by conduction to cook it right through to the centre. When cooking stews, casseroles and other dishes which require that various meats and vegetables be cooked together, make sure the ingredients are cut into the same shapes and sizes. This prevents the smaller pieces being *overcooked* before the larger pieces are cooked at all.

The shape of the food also affects cooking times. Whole poultry cooks more evenly if it is well trussed. Small protruding pieces such as the tips of wings and legs of poultry, or the narrower end of a leg of lamb may be wrapped with small smooth pieces of aluminium foil to reflect the microwaves away from these areas, and so slow down their cooking rate. The foil, of course, must never touch the sides of the oven interior, as this could cause arcing. Other foods or food portions may be uneven in shape—for instance, cauliflower, broccoli, lamb chops or whole fish. Since the thinner parts of these unevenly shaped foods will cook more quickly, it is

1 The thicker parts of unevenly-shaped foods, such as salmon steaks, should be placed towards the outside of the dish where the microwaves penetrate first.

2 Wrap small protruding pieces of otherwise uniformly-shaped joints and poultry with small pieces of aluminium foil to reflect microwaves away from this area and slow down their cooking rate.

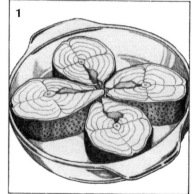
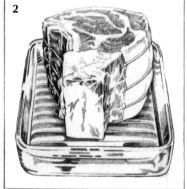

essential to place the thick portions of the food towards the outside of the dish, where the microwaves penetrate first. Although, as already mentioned, joints of meat on the bone win on cooking time, boned and rolled joints are preferable since their even shape ensures even cooking.

Quality of Raw Ingredients

The microwave oven does not have any magical powers to make inferior food taste superior. Just as with conventional cooking methods, end results will be affected by the quality of the raw ingredients used. For best results always use good quality foods, remembering that your microwave oven is a wonderful appliance, but that it cannot work miracles with poor quality foods or ingredients.

Moisture Content of Food

Always add the minimum amount of water when cooking vegetables, whether fresh or frozen. Adding more water slows down cooking, and should only be used for example if you wish to extend the cooking time or soften the vegetables. Foods which do not contain much moisture do not cook as satisfactorily in a microwave oven as those which do, since it is the water molecules which attract the microwaves.

Defrosting

When defrosting in a microwave oven it is essential that the ice is melted slowly, so that the food does not begin to cook on the outside before it is completely defrosted through to the centre. To prevent this happening food must be allowed to 'rest' between bursts of microwave energy. The 'defrost' setting on some microwave ovens does this automatically by pulsing the energy on and off. This can also be done by hand if your oven does not have an automatic defrost control. Larger, denser items of food such as joints of meat and frozen poultry do need to stand for a certain amount of time after defrosting in the oven to ensure that all the ice crystals have melted. During this standing time heat from the thawed outer layers will penetrate to the centre.

Reheating

Previously-cooked food can be quickly reheated in a microwave oven without excessive drying or loss of flavour, but care must be taken when reheating baked foods like rolls, mince pies, dough-nuts and so on, as these only take a few seconds and can be spoiled very easily by overheating. Foods which are denser, such as stews and casseroles, have to be stirred or re-arranged about half way through the heating time, or allowed a rest period afterwards, so that the centre is properly heated without over-heating the edges or outside.

Partly-cooked Foods

Partly-cooked foods, such as frozen vegetables which have been blanched before freezing, require a shorter cooking time than fresh vegetables, even from their frozen state. Some types of frozen vegetables need very little actual cooking time by any method of cooking, and really only require to be defrosted and heated through.

Cooking Techniques for Microwave Cooking

Most techniques used in microwave cooking are similar to those used in conventional cooking, but the method of application may be slightly different. The speed of microwave cooking means some of these special methods have to be followed carefully to ensure best results, whether you are defrosting, heating or cooking. Because of the way microwaves cook food (see pages 11–12) many recipes call for turning or stirring of food, standing time after cooking, special arrangement and re-arrangement of food during cooking, and careful covering or wrapping. Experience will serve as your best guide as you become familiar with these microwave cooking techniques.

1 Because food cooks from the outer edges inwards in a microwave oven, stirring dishes from the outside towards the centre during cooking will help produce even results.

2 Foods which cannot be stirred, such as cakes, should be turned over or round during cooking.

Stirring and Turning

Since the outer edges of food normally cook first in a microwave oven, stirring food during the cooking period helps to equalise the temperature in the food and produces more even results in a shorter time. Always stir from the outside of the dish, bringing the outer cooked portions towards the centre. Foods which are cooked whole—joints of meat, poultry or whole cauliflower, for example—should be turned over during the cooking period. Sometimes it is advisable to turn the cooking dish round during cooking, especially in ovens without a turntable.

Standing Time

Food continues to cook after it has been removed from a microwave oven, or when the microwave energy has been switched off. It is no longer being cooked by microwave energy but by the conduction of heat towards the centre. The period during which this happens is known as the 'standing time' and is sometimes necessary to complete the actual cooking process. The length of standing time recommended depends on the volume and density of the food. Sometimes it can be as short as the time it takes to remove the food from the oven and place it on the serving table, but larger, denser foods require a longer standing time. Sometimes you might be advised to undercook or underthaw foods slightly and allow the process to finish during the standing time—recipes recommend standing times when they are necessary. After standing for five to ten minutes, the internal temperature of many foods rises and finishes the cooking or heating process, so it is often most important to undercook and test for readiness *after* the standing time. Remember there is no remedy for overcooked food.

Arrangement of Food

Correct food arrangement is important for even defrosting, heating or cooking in a microwave oven. Always place the thicker or denser parts of the food towards the outside of the dish and the more easily heated thinner or more porous parts towards the centre of the dish. For example, when cooking chicken drumsticks, the thicker meatier parts are placed towards the outside of the dish with the thinner boned ends towards the centre. Cooking is most successful when the food is arranged so there is actually an empty space in the middle, such as a cake mixture cooked in a ring mould, or several individual portions or small dishes arranged in a circle inside the oven—the 'hole' left in the centre provides a greater area of outer edges and allows the microwaves to act more efficiently in the oven. Custards cooked in individual ramekins, for example, can be arranged in a circle directly on the oven floor. Jacket potatoes can be arranged in the same way—but do not place a potato in the centre. Individual items are also best spaced out, rather than placed close together, which again provides more

1 Whether cooking or defrosting chicken drumsticks arrange them so that the thinner bonier ends are towards the centre and the meatier parts are on the outside.

2 Arranging food in a circle with the centre left empty, will produce the most satisfactory results in a microwave cooker. This method should be used for meat balls, individual ramekins and potatoes.

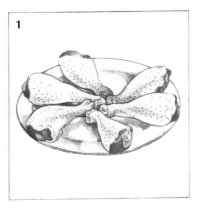

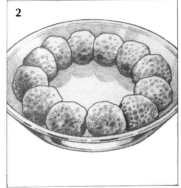

surface area. For even cooking, food should be arranged to a fairly similar depth too, so spread out peas, for example, in an even layer, rather than have a mound of peas in the centre of the dish. Similarly, when reheating a full meal already on a plate, try to keep the food at the same level, remembering to position the denser, thicker food around the outside of the plate and the thinner more porous foods towards the centre.

1 To encourage even cooking of food such as peas, arrange them in a layer of uniform depth, rather than heaped up towards the centre.

2 More even results can be produced by re-arranging items, such as meat balls, during cooking. Move those on the outside to the centre, and vice versa.

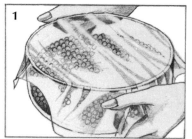
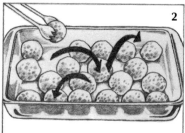

Re-arranging Food

When cooking or baking conventionally, some foods are often re-arranged during the cooking period, usually by altering the position of the cooking pot or turning the food in it. The same goes for microwave cooking. For instance, a dish of meatballs would be re-arranged during the cooking period, moving those which are cooking more quickly around the outside of the dish towards the centre, and those from the centre to the outside of the dish. Like stirring or turning, this gives more evenly cooked results in a shorter cooking time.

Covering Food

Just as putting a lid on a casserole when cooking conventionally retains steam and moisture to tenderise the meat, so many foods cook more quickly and evenly in the microwave oven if they are covered. Some foods require a tight fitting cover, while others prefer a covering which allows some moisture to escape. Vegetables are a good example. If they are covered with cling film, which forms a tight seal, they will cook more quickly and evenly than if a less efficient covering, such as a loose casserole lid, is used.

Most recipes indicate whether food should be covered or uncovered during microwave cooking. To avoid steam burns, always remove tight fitting lids or cling film carefully at the end of the cooking period.

Wrapping Food

When heating beefburgers or hot dogs in rolls, refreshing pastries, or thawing yeast dough items such as bread or bread rolls, you will find you get a better result if you wrap them loosely in a paper napkin or kitchen paper towel. Of course, porous items, such as bread and pastry, heat extremely quickly in a microwave oven and you should not leave the oven unattended while heating them through in case you overheat them.

Single Small Load

When heating a single small item, such as a rasher of bacon or one potato, all the microwave energy is concentrated on it. Cooking time is short, but some turning and manipulation is necessary to ensure even cooking results.

Cooking Equipment

You don't have to rush out and buy a complete new range of cooking equipment to use with your microwave oven. Many of the dishes and utensils you already have in your kitchen will be quite suitable. You won't be using your metal saucepans, metal baking tins or trays in your microwave oven, but you will be using some things which you have never used before as cooking utensils— such as paper plates, paper napkins and kitchen paper towel. You will often be able to cook and serve in the same dish or on the same plate, saving not only time but washing up too, and—just think—this means that there are no more dirty saucepans with baked on food to soak, scrub and clean afterwards either.

How to Test Cooking Containers and Utensils

Always carry out this simple test on containers, dishes or utensils before you use them in your microwave oven if you're not sure about their suitability or efficiency. Place the dish in the oven, together with a glass half full of water and set your microwave oven to cook on full power for about one minute. At the end of this time the water should be warm and the dish cool. If both are warm the dish can still be used but food will take longer to cook in it. If on the other hand the dish is hot and the water is cold, this means that the dish has been absorbing microwave energy and must not be used in the oven.

Heat Retention

Many dishes remain relatively cool during cooking in a microwave oven because microwaves pass straight through them and are absorbed by the food. However, as the food itself is hot, a certain amount of heat will be conducted from the food to the dish, so it is advisable to exercise care when removing it from the oven at the end of the cooking period. The amount of heat conducted to the dish will be influenced by several factors such as the type of food being cooked, the heating or cooking process and the length of time it is in the oven. Foods which have a high fat and sugar content can reach particularly high temperatures very quickly.

Microwave browning dishes which are specially designed to absorb microwave energy become very hot and should not be handled without the protection of oven gloves.

Unsuitable Containers

Metal Because it reflects microwaves, never use dishes or utensils with any form of metal trim, metal decoration or signature in a microwave oven. The metal content may cause arcing and damage both the dish and the oven magnetron. If a dish 'sparks' due to arcing when you are testing it, the oven should be switched off immediately. Sparks indicate that there is some metal content in the material used to make the dish, so it should not be used in a microwave oven.

Melamine and Tupperware Do not use melamine or Tupperware containers; these absorb microwaves and food doesn't cook in them.

Glued Containers Dishes or containers which have been repaired with glue, or have glued handles, should not be used, since the glue may melt.

Suitable Containers

The best containers to use are those which transmit microwaves, are non-porous and will not melt or warp.

Glass Oven-proof glass and glass-ceramic dishes (without metal trim) are the commonest microwave containers. Clear glass dishes,

Oven-proof glass and glass-ceramic containers are ideal for microwave use. Not only · do they allow the microwaves to pass straight through to the food, but, with the clear dishes, you can watch the food cooking in the dish. From the top left, clockwise: soufflé dish, ring mould, mixing bowl, measuring jug and, in the centre, a flan dish.

Cakes: from top to bottom, Lemon and Hazelnut Cake (page 100), Rich Fruit Cake (page 100) and Moist Chocolate Sandwich Cake (page 99).

such as Pyrex ware, are especially suitable for those unused to cooking with a microwave oven, because you can actually watch the food heating and cooking in the dish, and you can inspect the bases of cakes, pastries and puddings to see if they are cooked in the centre before turning out. Glass measuring jugs are particularly useful and often allow you to measure, mix and cook in the same container. Oven-proof glass and glass-ceramic dishes can also be used in conventional ovens and in freezers which makes them particularly versatile. Ordinary glass without any lead content may be used for short-term heating and cooking of foods which do not contain much fat or sugar, as the very high temperature reached when fat or sugar is heated could cause the glass to crack.

China and Pottery Sturdy china and pottery dishes without metal trim or content are usually suitable for microwave cookery. However, unglazed earthenware or pottery may be absorbent and should not be used. Any moisture present in them would absorb microwave energy, leaving less to cook the food. If you try the water test with porous earthenware or pottery you will find they become warm.

Clay Pots Clay will also transmit a certain level of microwaves. Use clay cooking pots or 'bricks' to tenderise meat casseroles as well as to cook joints of meat and whole poultry. The base and lid of the pot should be pre-soaked in water, according to the manufacturer's instructions. This moisture content will then absorb some

Pottery, clay and china utensils, which have been glazed, are all suitable for use inside a microwave oven. Unglazed ware has a tendency to absorb microwaves and prevent them from reaching the food. In dishes which require cooking more slowly, such as a meat casserole or roast chicken, this can be used to advantage by cooking in a pre-soaked clay brick. From the top left, clockwise: dinner plates, ramekin dishes, mugs, chicken brick and tea cup and saucer.

Desserts: from top to bottom, Stuffed Baked Apples (page 97) and Jam-Capped Suet Pudding (page 97) served with Custard Sauce (page 102).

microwave energy which in turn slows down the cooking rate and extends the cooking time. Since they do absorb some microwave energy, these pots will become hot during cooking. Rapid changes in temperature can cause the pots to crack, so be careful not to add very cold liquid during the cooking period.

Plastics Dishwasher-safe, boilable, rigid plastic containers are normally suitable for microwave use but preferably only for shorter cooking times. Those which can be taken direct from freezer to microwave are particularly handy. Highly coloured foods, such as baked beans in tomato sauce, tend to discolour some plastic containers during their microwave heating period. It is not advisable to use plastic containers for foods with a high fat or sugar content as the very high temperature may cause distortion or melting. Melamine is not recommended, neither is Tupperware. Since there is an ever increasing variety of plastics and plastic ware coming on to the market, you must follow each manufacturer's instructions carefully, as well as carrying out a short container test for about fifteen to twenty seconds, before using any new plastic container in a microwave oven. During or after the test, see if there is any discernible smell coming from the plastic which would of course make it unsuitable for cooking.

Plastic Foam Plastic foam cups and dishes may be used for short term heating, but not for cooking, as they would melt.

Plastic Baby Bottles can be used to warm milk gently.

Cling Film makes a good tight seal when used to cover cooking dishes. It should however be slit or pierced before its removal from a dish at the end of heating or cooking to avoid steam burns. Microwave-strength cling film is slightly tougher than ordinary cling film and less likely to burst during cooking. It has the additional advantage of sticking to plastic as well as glass and china and is sufficiently flexible when hot to be able to uncover and recover dishes during cooking. Do not use cling film which has foil edges.

Plastic Cooking Pouches, such as those containing commercially prepared foods, can be used to defrost, heat or cook the contents. They should be slit or pierced before placing in the microwave oven to allow steam to escape and prevent them from bursting.

Plastic Cooking Bags are also suitable for heating and cooking food, but these should also be pierced or slit before placing in the oven. Do not use the metal ties often supplied to seal the bags, use string or elastic bands instead.

Paper Paper can be used for short cooking times, but prolonged use in a microwave oven could cause it to burn. Do not line the

Articles made of paper, wood and straw can be used, with discretion, in a microwave cooker. But heat sensitive materials should only be used for reheating and warming up unless they are labelled otherwise.

oven with paper. Paper and card are useful for putting food on when defrosting or reheating pastry or bread items, or cooking jacket potatoes. Paper cups, cartons, plates, absorbent kitchen paper, greaseproof paper and plain white paper napkins (not coloured or patterned ones as the dye could be transferred to the food or floor of the oven) are all suitable. Paper board containers designed for oven use can be placed in any type of oven and are also freezer-proof. Some manufacturers of plastic covered paper plates and dishes are now labelling their products as suitable for microwave oven use. Always follow the manufacturers' recommendations, because some wax or plastic coated paper plates may melt if used in the oven.

Wood Wood contains water which will evaporate during microwave cooking and eventually cause it to dry and crack. However, small wooden utensils, such as wooden spoons, can withstand short periods in the oven.

Straw Straw and wicker baskets can be used for very short periods in the oven, for instance when reheating bread rolls which only require a few seconds of microwave energy.

Pure Cotton and Linen Napkins These can be used to line bread baskets or food to be warmed, or indeed if warm napkins are required. Their duration in the microwave oven should be brief, and napkins containing any synthetic fibres must not be used.

Metal Utensils made of metal, containing metal, or which have a metal trim should never be used in a microwave oven. Metal reflects microwaves, inhibits cooking and can damage the utensil as well as the magnetron tube which would overheat and have a shortened life. Metal rims and signatures on dishes will darken and could cause the dish to crack. Some dairy products such as butter and cream cheese are purchased in aluminium foil or foil-lined wrappings. Do not try to defrost or heat them before removing them from their wrappers. There are, as always, exceptions to the rules and these are listed below, but in any situation which allows the use of metal inside the oven, the metal must never touch the interior surfaces since this can cause arcing or pitting of the oven interior.

1 Foil 'TV dinner' trays less than 2 cm ($\frac{3}{4}$ inch) deep can be used because they are shallow enough to allow microwave energy to penetrate and heat the food from the top.
2 Small pieces of smooth aluminium foil can be used to shield parts of food, or to slow down cooking. The thinner ends of joints of meat or fish, the tips of poultry wings or legs, or the outside edges of food can all be covered in this way. The foil must never touch the interior surfaces of the oven.
3 Metal skewers or clamps may be used when the proportion of food is much greater than the amount of metal. For instance, you can defrost a commercially frozen chicken or turkey in its original bag with metal clamp closure, provided the metal does not touch the oven interior. Metal twist ties supplied with cooking bags should not be used in the oven; replace them with string or elastic bands.

Special Microwave Cookware and Accessories

There is an ever-increasing variety of cookware and accessories on the market specially designed for use in microwave ovens. You can buy ring moulds, pudding basins, loaf and cake dishes, casseroles, trays and divided trays, stacking rings, pie plates, dessert bowls, muffin pans, ramekin and soufflé dishes. Some are disposable, such as containers made of soft plastics, paper, paperboard, pressed polystyrene or bags, such as boil-in-bags, roasting bags and cling film. Others are semi-disposable, being made of semi-soft plastics, whilst many are designed for permanent use and are made of hard plastics, glass or earthenware.

Some can also be used, within certain temperatures, in a conventional oven and many are safe for use in a dishwasher and in a freezer as well. Always follow the manufacturer's instructions

The range of bakeware designed specially for use in a microwave cooker is very wide, ranging from the cheap and disposable to the more permanent varieties. From top left, clockwise we have selected the following: bun tray, roasting rack, dual vegetable dish, ring mould and, in the centre, a baking tray.

and recommendations for use, because some of these containers can only be used in relatively low temperatures or for foods which never get hotter than the boiling point of water (100°C/212°F). They must not be used over prolonged heating periods or to cook foods with a high fat or sugar content which would cause them to melt or distort.

As well as specialised containers you can also purchase special microwave cooking accessories such as bacon racks, roasting racks, browning grills or skillets, meat thermometers and even portable turntables.

Microwave Thermometers Ordinary thermometers must not be used in a microwave oven as the mercury is affected by microwave energy. Specially designed meat thermometers which can be used in a microwave oven during cooking are now available, and should be used in accordance with the manufacturer's instructions. Conventional meat thermometers can only be inserted in meat *after* it has been removed from the oven. Some microwave ovens have a built-in temperature sensing probe, which can be inserted into roasts or other foods during cooking. When the food reaches the pre-set temperature the oven automatically switches off or reduces the power level to keep the food warm until it is removed from the oven.

Microwave Browning Grills or Skillets Many foods, especially meats, cook too fast in microwave ovens for them to brown properly, so they can look unappetising. However, special browning dishes have been developed to get round this problem. They are made of glass ceramic with a special tin oxide coating on their undersides which absorbs microwave energy when they are preheated empty in the oven. The base of the empty dish becomes very hot so the outside of food placed on the surface is seared and browned, while the rest is cooked through by microwave energy. The food is usually turned over during the cooking period to brown the other side. Browning dishes are ideal for foods which are normally grilled or fried, such as steak, chops, beefburgers, sausages, chicken portions, some fish, and for toasted or grilled sandwiches. Preheating times will vary depending on the size and shape of the browning dish, the particular microwave oven used, the type of food being cooked and personal preference. Always use oven gloves when handling browning dishes as they do get very hot. Also protect your kitchen work surface or table before placing these dishes on them. Follow the manufacturer's instructions for their use, care and cleaning.

Microwave Roasting Racks Roasting racks are specially designed for use in a microwave oven and may be made of a ceramic or hard plastic material. They are used to raise meats and poultry above their own juices during cooking, and can also be used for heating bread and bread products such as rolls.

The Best Size and Shape of Cooking Container

In a microwave oven the container you use is almost as important as the food you cook in it. The size and shape of the dish influences how the food cooks, the amount of attention it requires during the cooking period, as well as the time taken to cook the food.

Size

1 The size of the cooking dish should match the amount of food. If the dish is too small, spillage is inevitable, especially when cooking foods which tend to boil up or bubble during cooking, such as recipes with a water or milk base, when the dish should only be about half to two thirds full. If, on the other hand, the container is too big in relation to the amount of food, any thinner, liquid parts will spread out and overcook because more microwave energy reaches them over the larger surface area.

Shape

The shape of the dish is more critical when cooking in a microwave oven than in conventional cooking.

1 The same amount of stew will take longer to cook in a small, deep dish (above) than in a wide, shallow dish (below). This is because there is a greater surface area exposed to microwave energy in a shallower dish.

2 A ring mould, with its empty central area, is the best shape of container for use, where appropriate, in a microwave oven. Construct your own by placing a glass tumbler in the centre of a round, shallow dish.

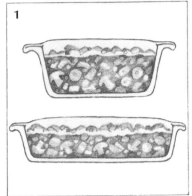

1 The depth of the dish affects how the food cooks and the length of time required. The same amount of food will take longer to cook in a narrow, deeper dish than it would in a wider, shallow dish because the latter type exposes a greater food surface area to microwave energy. Use a deep casserole when cooking large quantities of food which need to be simmered or require stirring during cooking, and a shallow dish for foods which do not require to be stirred, or for heating leftovers which cannot be stirred or rearranged during reheating.

2 For most even heating and cooking, the rounder the dish the better. Next best are oval and square dishes, and rectangular dishes are the least efficient. Both square and rectangular containers should have rounded corners. Sharp corners allow more exposure to microwaves and can cause food to dry out or overcook in these areas before the centre is cooked.

3 Straight-sided dishes are preferable to those with sloping or curved sides. This is because in the very areas where most of the microwave energy is received, on the outside, the food is less deep and is therefore in greater danger of overcooking. Straight-sided dishes provide a uniform depth of food.

4 The shape of the dish should follow the shape of the food. Try to avoid extra dish space around the food, especially when defrosting or when cooking bulky foods with very little liquid, like vegetables.

5 Ring moulds, so long as they aren't metal, are excellent for heating or cooking foods which cannot be stirred to equalise temperature during their time in the microwave oven. They are particularly good for cakes and desserts because they allow microwaves to penetrate the food from the centre as well as the sides, top and bottom. A glass tumbler placed in the centre of a round dish makes a good substitute for a ring mould.

Always use the size and shape of dish recommended in a recipe, otherwise timing and results may vary.

When to Cook with a Cover

Covering food shortens the cooking time, retains moisture, promotes even cooking, tenderises, and prevents splashing in a microwave oven, just like conventional cooking. As a general rule, food is covered when moisture is to be retained during defrosting, heating or cooking by microwave energy (for example, soups, casseroles, vegetables). On the other hand, foods which should be dry, such as cakes, bread and pastry, are not normally covered. If a recipe recommends that food should be covered, this will usually be in the form of a loose, perhaps absorbent cover, such as absorbent kitchen paper. Most recipes indicate whether or not food should be covered in microwave cooking and obviously these recommendations should be followed for satisfactory results. If no cover is specified, assume that the food is uncovered. Always use the type of covering recommended either below, or within a particular recipe.

Cling Film

This provides a tight cover which retains heat and moisture to tenderise and cook food more quickly. It is frequently used in microwave cooking to cover meat and poultry dishes, rice and pasta, uncoated fish, stewed fruit and vegetables. It can also be used to wrap some individual vegetables, such as small whole beetroot, during cooking. Before removing it from a dish either during or at the end of a cooking period, it must first be pierced to allow steam to escape and prevent steam burns on the hands.

Lids

Clear ovenproof glass or casserole lids without metal trim can also be used to retain moisture during cooking. Alternatively you can substitute an upturned plate made of ovenproof china or glass. Always remove lids very carefully, tipping them away from you, to prevent burns from the steam trapped underneath.

Paper

Dry paper absorbs moisture, and is useful to prevent bread, bread products, cakes and pastry from becoming soggy, especially during reheating in a microwave oven. Do not overheat food in paper and do not line the oven with paper. Absorbent kitchen paper and plain white unpatterned paper napkins can be used to cover bacon or foods which tend to spit and splash fat on to the oven interior. Greaseproof paper also forms a loose cover, and is used to retain heat and prevent spitting on foods which do not require to have steam retained to tenderise them. Corn on the cob can be cooked in the oven by wrapping in buttered greaseproof paper and placing on a serving plate.

Roasting Bags

These are useful aids to encourage browning when roasting meat and poultry. Do ensure that the bag is pierced or slit in two or three places to allow steam to escape during cooking. Tie the end of the bag loosely with string or an elastic band, and do not use the metal ties often supplied with these bags.

What Happens to Foods in your Microwave Oven

Some foods will retain more natural colour and have more flavour than when cooked conventionally, while some others will not brown or crisp. As with any cooking medium, the end results will always depend on the initial quality of the raw food.

Fish and Seafood

These cook to perfection in a microwave oven. Fresh or frozen, they have a delicate flavour with tender flaky flesh which remains moist due to the absence of dry heat. Commercially frozen individual fish portions in sauce can be cooked quickly from their frozen state in their original plastic pouches, which only require to be pierced or slit on top. Placing such pouches in a dish while cooking will avoid the possibility of any leakage on the oven surface.

Roast Meats

Meat can be roasted in a microwave oven, but browning will depend on the weight of the joint. Small joints weighing 1.35 kg (3 lb) or less cook too quickly to allow them time to brown, although the use of pierced roasting bags, tied with string or elastic bands, does encourage browning. They will however look different from conventionally roasted joints of meat and will not generally be crisp on the outside, though the flesh will be tender and juicy. If you intend to serve roast potatoes and/or Yorkshire pudding with the meat, it makes sense to cook the joint with them conventionally, using the microwave oven to cook the accompanying vegetables, sauces and perhaps a dessert.

The flavour of microwaved meat may be a little different. This is due to the retention of juices.

Casseroles

Casseroles using the cheaper cuts of meat do really need to be cooked on a low power setting in a microwave oven, in order to slow down the rate of cooking and allow time for the tougher meat fibres to tenderise and for flavours to mingle and develop. Meat casseroles are more tender and tasty if they are cooked the previous day and reheated gently when required, rather than served immediately after cooking.

Steak, Chops, Sausages and Beefburgers

These will not brown in a microwave oven unless they are seared and cooked on a browning dish. Breadcrumb coatings will not be as crisp as when grilled or fried conventionally, due to steam rising from the food.

Bacon Rashers and Joints

Bacon rashers placed between the folds of absorbent kitchen paper will brown and crisp because of their high fat content. Uncooked bacon joints are best cooked in pierced roasting bags. Unsmoked joints are preferable to smoked, since the latter's higher salt content can cause slight dehydration and hardening of the outer surfaces. Pre-cooked bacon joints are quickly heated through in a microwave oven.

Meat Loaves and Meatballs

These cook well by microwave energy and more quickly than by conventional methods. Meat loaves are tender and juicy but do not crisp as much on the outside as when cooked in a conventional oven. Small meat balls cook in minutes.

Meat Pies

Double crust pastry pies should be baked in a conventional oven, since they must be crisp and brown. Single crust pies can be acceptable in a microwave oven if the pastry base is cooked first either conventionally or by microwaves, before adding the filling. Suet pastry meat pies or puddings can be cooked successfully in the microwave oven, as can meat and vegetable pies with potato toppings. Pre-cooked pastry pies can be quickly reheated by microwaves, and should be placed on absorbent kitchen paper to absorb moisture.

Poultry and Game

Poultry and game can be cooked most successfully. The cooked meat will be juicy and tender but, like red meat, browning will depend on weight and time taken to cook. For instance, a large turkey will brown far more than a chicken, due to the longer cooking time. Again, pierced roasting bags, tied with string or elastic bands, encourage browning of smaller birds. The skin will be soft, but a few minutes under a grill or in a hot conventional oven will soon crispen this if desirable. Poultry portions can also be cooked very quickly, and will remain moist.

Rice and Pasta

Rice and pasta cooked by microwave energy still need time to absorb moisture and rehydrate. For this reason there is little or no time saving compared with conventional cooking methods, but they can often be cooked and served in the same dish, the kitchen is not filled with steam, nor are there any sticky saucepans to clean afterwards. Reheating cooked rice or pasta, whether refrigerated or frozen, is no longer a problem with a microwave cooker; rice reheated in a microwave oven is especially light and fluffy.

Sauces

Sauces, whether sweet or savoury, are a pleasure to make in a microwave oven. No more burning or sticking to the base of a saucepan, and, with occasional stirring, no more lumps. They look and taste as good as, if not better than, conventionally cooked sauces and can often be cooked in the serving jug or boat.

Eggs and Cheese

Since microwaves are attracted to the fat in the egg yolk, it cooks before the white. After breaking the egg into the dish or cup in which you are cooking it, the yolk should be carefully pricked with a wooden cocktail stick or the tines of a fork to puncture the surrounding membrane before cooking. Eggs can be poached or baked in the shortest possible time and look and taste like those cooked conventionally but, as already mentioned, eggs should not be cooked in their shells in a microwave oven. Fried eggs can be cooked in the special browning dish or grill. Scrambled eggs, with or without butter added, are fluffier and lighter and there is no crusty saucepan to clean. Cheese melts and cooks rapidly, giving a quick attractive finish to many dishes. To brown a cheese topping, simply place the dish under a pre-heated conventional grill for a few minutes after cooking in the microwave oven.

Cakes, Bread, Biscuits and Pastry

Cakes cook quickly and rise higher in a microwave oven but of course they do not brown. For the greatest eye appeal, choose recipes which are dark in colour such as chocolate, coffee, gingerbread, spiced or dark fruit cakes. Lighter coloured cakes can be suitably iced or decorated.

Bread can be proved and cooked in a microwave oven, but will not have the characteristic crisp crust or baked appearance of conventionally baked bread. The outside of the bread can of course be browned and crisped after cooking if placed under a hot grill or in a hot oven for a few minutes. The use of wholemeal or wholewheat flour enhances the overall appearance.

Some cookie type biscuits can be cooked successfully, but the more traditional type crisp biscuits must be baked conventionally. As already mentioned, double crust pastry pies cannot be cooked by microwave though shortcrust pastry is satisfactory when used for the base of a quiche. Suet pastry benefits from the moistness of microwave cookery. Frozen cakes, bread, biscuits and pastry can be quickly defrosted in a microwave oven.

Sandwiches and Yeast Products

Sandwiches and bread rolls often taste better when warm. They are porous foods which heat extremely quickly and must not be overheated because the bread will toughen. Bread rolls heat in seconds rather than minutes—one bread roll in 10 seconds. The same applies to other yeast products including jam doughnuts—never bite into a jam doughnut immediately after reheating it even for only a few seconds in a microwave oven, because, although it may feel barely warm on the outside, the jam inside may be hot enough to burn your tongue. Always allow the doughnut to stand for a few minutes before removing it from the oven to allow the heat to equalise before serving. Conventionally toasted bread is preferable to untoasted bread when making sandwiches in a microwave oven. Place sandwiches and bread products on absorbent kitchen paper or napkins to absorb moisture, and do not leave the oven unattended during the short heating period.

Appetisers and Dips

Do not assemble canapés until ready to heat, otherwise the toast or biscuit base will be soggy. Pastry bases or cases for appetisers should be baked conventionally to crisp and brown them. Hot dips are easy and quick to make in a microwave oven and do not stick or burn as they sometimes do when cooked conventionally. The same applies to fondues which are ideal for microwave cookery.

Preserves

Jams, marmalades and chutneys can all be cooked in a microwave oven. They require less attention than when cooked conventionally and do not stick to the bottom of the container. The bowl or container used must be at least two to three times as large as the amount of chutney or preserve being made to allow for 'boiling up' and to prevent spillage. Microwave ovens are particularly useful for making small batches of preserves.

Toffee and Fudge

Both these are suitable for microwave cooking and will not stick or burn but, like preserves, they must be cooked in a large bowl or container which is at least two to three times as big as the amount of mixture to allow for 'boiling up'.

Vegetables and Fruit

Vegetables retain their natural colour and flavour and are crisp but tender. Since they are cooked in very little water—some don't require any water at all—there is maximum vitamin and nutrient retention. Fruits are juicy and tender and dried fruits such as prunes do not require to be soaked overnight before cooking by microwaves.

Leftovers

Leftovers reheated in a microwave oven look and taste freshly cooked and do not dry up as when kept warm or reheated by conventional methods.

Frozen Foods

Most will reheat quickly and satisfactorily by microwaves. Use a dish of the same shape and size as the frozen food to prevent the overcooking of melted parts. Crumb coated or topped foods will not be crisp, but can, if preferred, be browned and crisped on top afterwards under a pre-heated grill.

How to Improve the Appearance of Microwaved Food

Most people who have not used a microwave oven are concerned about how food will look when it is cooked. However, as soon as they become accustomed to microwave cooking, many owners agree that browning, or rather the lack of it, is not as important as they thought it would be. There are, however, ways in which food can be given the traditional appearance of conventional cooking methods.

Meat and Poultry

For instance small chickens, chicken portions or small pieces of meat can be brushed with melted butter and sprinkled with paprika before cooking, or they can be coated with a mixture of butter and brown sauce, Worcestershire, barbecue or soy sauce. Alternatively, you can sprinkle herbs, crumbled beef stock cubes or dry soup mix, such as onion, on top before cooking, and basting with fat during cooking also helps. Ham and poultry can be glazed with marmalade and other preserves as in conventional recipes, after half the cooking time. Accompanying sauces also add interest to the final appearance. Main course dishes such as casseroles are enhanced when sprinkled with browned breadcrumbs with or without Parmesan cheese, or crushed potato crisps after the final stirring. Crumbled cooked bacon or grated cheese can be added either before cooking or after the final stirring.

Cakes and Bread

Cakes are often iced or decorated before serving, so lack of browning on them is not noticeable. However, if an alternative cake topping is preferred, a mixture of cinnamon and sugar or cinnamon and coconut can be sprinkled on top before cooking. Chopped nuts or a mixture of chopped nuts and soft brown sugar can either be sprinkled on the top surface after half the cooking time, or at the end of the cooking period and before standing. Bread and bread rolls can be brushed with beaten egg or milk and sprinkled with poppy seeds or cracked wheat before cooking. They can of course be browned for a few minutes under a grill after their removal from the microwave oven. If you brown them in their microwave cooking containers, do make sure that these will withstand the heat of a radiant grill. Using brown flour and brown sugar adds colour to bread, cakes and pastry and is well worth trying.

How to Test When Food is Cooked

Although the appearance of some foods cooked by microwaves will differ from those cooked conventionally, many of the tests for readiness are the same. Personal preferences will dictate to a certain extent the degree of readiness—some people will prefer foods more 'well done' than others—so cooking times will have to be adjusted accordingly. There are, however, ways of testing whether food is properly cooked through.

One of the most difficult things to learn about cooking by microwaves is when to remove the food from the oven. Many foods must be removed from the oven while they still look only partly cooked, to prevent overcooking during the standing time. Always undercook rather than risk overcooking until you become accustomed to cooking by microwaves and are familiar with how cooked food should look. Be patient and leave food to stand. If after the standing time it is not cooked to your liking, it can easily be returned to the oven for further cooking, but there is no magic remedy for overcooked, spoilt food.

Cakes and Sponge Puddings

A wooden cocktail stick inserted in the centre of the cake or pudding should come out clean. Small moist areas on the surface will dry during a few minutes standing time. The sides of the cake or pudding will pull away from the sides of the cooking container when it is cooked.

Egg-based Custards and Fillings

Baked egg custards and quiche fillings will still appear soft in the centre, but a knife inserted half way between the outer edge and the centre should come out clean. The centre will set during the standing time.

Fish

Fish should flake easily when cooked. It may still appear to be slightly translucent in the centre, but will cook through during the standing time. Shellfish will turn pink and opaque when cooked. Careful timing is essential to prevent overcooking, otherwise fish will be tough and dry.

Meat

The flesh should be tender when tested with a fork. Cheaper less tender cuts of meat should split at the fibres when cooked.

Standing time is essential for all meats whether joints of meat or casseroles, and helps to tenderise. Cover joints of meat with aluminium foil, shiny side in, during the standing time. It is a good idea to cook meat casseroles the day before they are required and then reheat gently the following day, stirring during the reheating period. This method of cooking does help to tenderise the meat. Always use a meat thermometer to check the internal temperature of joints of meat to ensure that they are cooked to the desired degree of readiness.

Remember only special microwave meat thermometers can be used in the oven during cooking, but a conventional meat thermometer can be inserted in the joint after it has been removed from the oven.

Poultry

Always use a microwave meat thermometer or a conventional meat thermometer to check internal temperature in the thickest parts of both thighs and the breast meat of whole poultry. The juices should also run clear without any trace of pinkish colour, and the drumsticks should move freely at the joints. As with meat, standing time after cooking is essential for all poultry dishes. Remember that because the meat continues to cook while standing, it should not be allowed to reach the desired internal temperature in the microwave oven but shortly after its removal. During the standing time, cover whole poultry (with the thermometer still inserted) under a tent of aluminium foil, shiny side in. The meat should also be tender to the touch of a fork.

Vegetables

These should be fork-tender, not mushy, when cooked. Jacket potatoes, however, will still feel firm when removed from the oven and if they were cut through the middle at this stage the centre would be uncooked. A standing time of approximately five minutes is essential before serving or cutting the potatoes. Do not overcook potatoes, and remember that they will hold their heat for up to about half an hour after cooking if they are wrapped in aluminium foil. This is useful to know when planning to cook a meal in the microwave oven and means that other foods can be cooked while the jacket potatoes retain their heat.

Single Crust Pastry Flan or Shell

Pastry should be flaky and puffy but will not brown, although a few brown spots may appear. The base should be dry and opaque.

Reheating Pre-Served Meals on Plates

Feel the bottom of the plate, especially the centre. When the food is hot enough to serve, the base of the plate will feel warm all over, having been heated by conduction from the hot food.

Using a Microwave Oven in Conjunction with a Conventional Cooker

A microwave oven used in conjunction with a conventional cooker offers the easiest and most efficient method of food preparation. Enjoy the speed of microwave cooking and complement it with the browning, grilling and dry heat baking advantages of your conventional cooker. Here are a few examples.

1 Partly cook chicken portions or pork ribs for barbecued dishes in the microwave oven, and finish on your outdoor barbecue or under your conventional grill. Any leftovers can be frozen and quickly reheated by microwaves, as and when required.

2 Cook the basic ingredients for au gratin and cheese-topped savoury dishes as well as crunchy or crumble-topped desserts with the speed of microwave, then crisp and brown the toppings under a conventional grill or in a conventional oven.

3 Retain moisture in whole poultry by cooking in the microwave oven, and then crisp and brown the skin under a conventional grill or in a conventional oven.

4 Bake savoury or sweet double crust pastry pies in a conventional oven, and reheat or defrost quickly by microwave energy.

5 Make pancakes or crêpes on a conventional cooker hob while the fillings are cooked in the microwave oven. Defrost or reheat filled crêpes by microwaves.

6 Use a conventional cooker hob to sear and brown meat or poultry and vegetables for stews and casseroles before cooking by microwaves.

7 Prove yeast doughs in the microwave oven and bake in a conventional oven to crust and brown the bread.

8 Toast bread conventionally but make or heat the fillings for toasted sandwiches in the microwave oven.

9 Bake flan cases conventionally if preferred, then add the filling—or cook the filling separately—and finish with the speed of microwave energy.

10 Soften hard sugar in its original wrappings on 'high' for 40 seconds.

11 Melt butter or chocolate for puddings or cakes in mixing bowl before adding other ingredients.

When foods are cooked by both microwave energy and conventional heat, be sure to select suitable cooking containers which will transmit microwave energy but which are also recommended for use with a conventional oven, grill or hob. Metal cooking pots should of course not be used in a microwave oven. Suitable containers will usually be either ovenproof, heat-tempered glass, ceramic—and of course some of the special microwave cookware can be used in a conventional oven within certain temperature limits. Always follow the manufacturer's recommendations and instructions for use.

Using a Microwave Oven with a Home Freezer

The ability to defrost foods in minutes rather than hours is one of the major advantages of owning a microwave oven. When freezing homemade foods which will be defrosted in the microwave oven, the following hints will be useful.

1 Freeze food in a container suitable for microwave oven use, so it can be defrosted, heated or cooked straight from the freezer. If you do not want to lose the use of a dish while the food is in the freezer, line the dish with freezer film or aluminium foil, arrange the food in the dish and freeze. Once frozen, turn the food out of the container, wrap it tightly, label and return to the freezer. When ready to use simply remove the freezer film or aluminium foil and return the food to the container before placing in the microwave oven. If you want to store food in the serving dish in the freezer just wrap the complete dish in freezer film or aluminium foil, or seal it in a large, heavy duty freezer bag. Remember to remove aluminium foil and metal ties before placing food or containers in a microwave oven.

2 Foods can be frozen in single portions so that any member of the family can quickly and easily defrost, heat or cook their own individual dish at any time. Similarly, before freezing a conventionally-baked double crust pie, pizza, quiche or flan, cut it into portions so that the required number of servings can be defrosted as required, rather than having, perhaps unnecessarily, to defrost them in their entirety.

3 Your own homemade TV snacks can be frozen on paperboard plates, ready to be placed in the microwave oven before serving.

4 To save time spent on food preparation, plan to cook extra food which can be frozen in dishes suitable for use in the microwave oven. These can then be reheated and ready to eat in minutes on a future occasion.

5 Complete main courses of cooked foods can be frozen on serving plates which are suitable for both freezing and for microwave oven use. Within minutes any member of the family can have a piping hot, ready-to-eat main course with all the trimmings! These can be particularly useful when one or both parents are away from home, leaving other members of the family behind to cater for themselves.

COOKING PRACTICE

The cooking of food, by any medium, is an art and requires patience, skill, talent, and creativity as well as common sense. Give any two people the same recipe and the same appliance to cook a specific dish and invariably the end results will differ, depending on the way both the recipe and the cooking appliance have been handled, the quality and variety of the ingredients used, as well as personal skill, style, judgement, taste and presentation.

Although you don't have to learn basic cookery all over again, cooking with a microwave is a different and very much quicker method of cooking, and one of the most difficult things you will have to appreciate is the speed of cooking. Just as you didn't learn conventional cooking methods in a day, neither can you expect to become a microwave cookery expert overnight.

Whether it's learning to ski, play golf, drive a car or even mastering a foreign language, the key to success is always patience and perseverance. The golden rule in microwave cooking is to be a clock watcher, and undercook rather than run the risk of overcooking food.

The need to underestimate rather than overestimate the defrosting, heating or cooking time cannot be stressed strongly enough. This is perhaps the most essential ingredient for success in microwave cooking. Watch food defrosting, heating or cooking in the oven, and do not be afraid to open the oven door to examine the food. Test frequently for readiness, and stir or turn the food or the dish as necessary during its time in the oven.

Do not try to be too ambitious too soon. Allow time to appreciate how quickly foods become heated and cooked. Don't try to cook a complete meal the first time you use the oven. Start with simple things. Make a cup of coffee, cook one or two jacket potatoes, try scrambled eggs, cooking bacon, reheating a meal already arranged on a plate or perhaps heating bread rolls.

Allow time to become familiar with microwave cooking before you try to roast a joint of meat or bake a cake, or cook a complete meal. To begin with, plan to cook perhaps one dish for each meal in the microwave oven, and continue to cook the other foods by normal conventional methods.

Above all, read the preceding pages in this book so you really understand why microwave cooking techniques have to be different. It won't be long before you are an expert too.

Menu Planning

When you have cooked a few simple foods in your microwave oven you will soon want to combine foods to make a meal. Since different foods cook in different ways and require different cooking times, foods are prepared and cooked in sequence.

To begin with, you may find that meals need a little more planning than when you cooked them conventionally but the time saved in meal preparation is well worth the time spent on planning. The following hints should prove useful.

1 Allow plenty of time when planning your first few meals so that you can take things step by step and won't feel rushed. Try to serve one cold course either as a starter or a dessert and use your microwave oven for the main course.

2 Complete meals, and certainly part of the meal, can be cooked several hours in advance, stored in a refrigerator, and reheated when required, because food reheated in a microwave oven has the appearance and flavour of freshly cooked food, and does not dry up. While eating one course, the next can be heating.

3 Many desserts can be cooked well in advance. They may require to be refrigerated or allowed time to set before serving. If they are served hot they are probably suitable for last minute cooking or a few seconds reheating while you are eating the main course.

4 Main course dishes which require standing time usually have the most flexibility and are cooked before the accompanying vegetables. Dense meat dishes such as joints and casseroles hold their heat well during their standing time, while the vegetables are being cooked.

5 Jacket potatoes cooked and wrapped in foil will keep warm for about half an hour after cooking.

6 Vegetables, apart from jacket potatoes, have limited flexibility, and while reheating is possible, some may become overcooked if reheated too often.

7 Soups, sauces and gravies can be prepared in advance, placed in serving dishes and reheated when required.

8 Fish dishes, especially those without sauce, do not hold their heat well.

9 Fish, seafood, egg and cheese dishes cook very quickly, making it difficult to reheat them without overcooking. It is therefore preferable to cook these dishes by microwave just before serving.

10 Since you cannot roast potatoes or bake Yorkshire pudding in a microwave oven, it makes sense to roast a joint of beef together with these in a conventional oven, leaving the microwave oven free to cook other foods such as the accompanying vegetables, sauces, dessert or starter.

11 Rice and pasta reheat quickly and most satisfactorily in a microwave oven, but require the same cooking time whether cooked conventionally or by microwave energy.

12 Wherever possible, cook food in the serving dish. This helps to retain heat during the standing time before serving. If the food has cooled slightly it can be returned to the microwave for a minute or two immediately prior to serving.

13 Bread and other yeast products such as bread rolls are usually the last item to be heated before the meal begins. They only require a few seconds to heat through, but lose their heat rapidly. Rolls will toughen or dry out if overheated.

14 Any single dish, portion of food or main course set out on a plate can be quickly reheated for or by the latecomer. Do not leave the microwave oven unattended during these short term reheating periods.

15 Watch food cook through the oven door and test, test, test frequently until you become accustomed to this new, very fast method of cooking. It isn't automatic—it still needs a cook to control it!

Adapting Conventional Recipes

It is not wise to try to adapt or convert recipes until you have mastered the basics of microwave cooking and are truly familiar with the performance of your microwave oven. Many of your favourite conventional recipes can no doubt be adapted to microwave cooking, sometimes with few changes other than a reduced cooking time. Obviously a general conversion chart to include individual family favourites is impossible, and as with any form of cooking, you will want to experiment and learn to use your microwave oven, adjusting cooking times, seasonings and flavourings to suit you and your family. The following guidelines will be of assistance.

1 Select foods which cook well by microwave. Since this is a moist form of cooking, most conventional recipes which are normally boiled, steamed, poached, covered or cooked in liquid will be found suitable.

2 It will usually be necessary to reduce the amount of liquid given in the conventional recipe by about one quarter. If necessary, more liquid can always be added during the cooking period.

3 Try to find a similar microwave recipe and use it as a guide, starting with the same amount of basic ingredients.

4 Foods which are naturally moist such as soups, sauces, fruit, vegetables, chicken portions and seafood are normally suitable, but will sometimes require less additional liquid than given in a conventional recipe. Many casseroles and foods cooked in sauce adapt easily to microwave cooking.

5 Generally foods cook in about one quarter to one third of the conventional cooking time—but as always, there are exceptions to any rule, and some foods will take even less, or more, time than this to cook.

6 Always underestimate the cooking time and test frequently for readiness. Remember that food will continue to cook by heat conduction after its removal from the cooker and during the standing time, so allowance must be made for this.

7 Reduce the amount of seasoning used, especially of those with strong flavours. Herbs and spices are more powerful in microwave cooking, since their flavours are not diluted. Further seasoning can be added, if necessary, after tasting and before serving.

8 Select cooking dishes which are larger than those specified in conventional recipes, to prevent spillage.

9 Containers used for cake and pudding mixtures which will rise during cooking, should not be filled more than one third to one half full of raw mixture.

Conventional Recipes which should NOT be Adapted to Microwave Cooking

1 Do not attempt deep fat frying in a microwave oven.

2 Do not cook eggs in their shell, or reheat whole already cooked shelled eggs.

3 Double crust pastry pies, pizzas, crusty bread, batter recipes such as pancakes and Yorkshire pudding, soufflés, meringues and meringue toppings, roast potatoes must all be cooked conventionally.

4 Uncooked rice, pasta and dried vegetables need time to absorb moisture and rehydrate just as they do for conventional cooking. If you try cooking them in a microwave oven but are following a conventional recipe, the rice or pasta may not be cooked in the time taken to cook other foods combined with them.

Defrosting Frozen Food

This is one of the major advantages of a microwave oven and most countertop portable models have a defrost or low setting which is used for this purpose.

The setting used in this book is referred to as 'low', and times are based on an approximate wattage of 200W–300W at this setting (i.e. 30%–50% of 600W–700W power output ovens).

If there is no defrost control on the oven, it can be simulated by turning the oven on to full power for 30 seconds and then off for $1\frac{1}{2}$ minutes. Repeat this until the frozen food is defrosted.

Times are approximate and should be used only as a guide, since they may vary, depending not only on the shape, density and weight of frozen food, but also the temperature at which it was stored in the freezer. Refer to the manufacturer's instruction manual for specific times for your particular oven.

Defrosting Guidelines

1 Always underestimate defrosting times. Many foods will still be icy in the centre when removed from the cooker, but will melt through during the standing time. If necessary, food can be returned to the microwave oven for further defrosting.

2 Remove metal twist ties from bags and replace with string or an elastic band before putting the bags in the oven.

3 Remove all lids from jars or containers.

4 Open cartons before placing them in the oven.

5 Slit or pierce plastic pouches or packaging.

6 If frozen food has to be placed in a dish, match the size and shape of dish to the size and shape of the food.

7 Food can be defrosted in foil trays which do not exceed 1.5 cm ($\frac{3}{4}$ inch) in depth.

8 For faster and more even defrosting, separate frozen foods, such as chops, into pieces as they thaw.

9 Turn food over if possible during defrosting. If this is not possible, rearrange individual items or turn the dish round.

10 Shake or gently break down fruit during the defrosting and standing time.

11 Flex pouches and packagings which cannot be broken up or stirred, to distribute the heat.

12 Pierce the skins of frozen foods such as frankfurters before defrosting.

13 Pour off liquid from poultry which has been frozen and is being defrosted in its original plastic bag. This liquid absorbs microwave energy and slows down the defrosting process.

14 Finish defrosting poultry in cold water in its original closed plastic bag, rather than try to completely defrost it with microwave energy, otherwise it may start to cook around the outside before it is fully thawed in the centre. Remember to remove giblets from defrosted poultry before cooking.

15 Fish, seafood and meat can also be defrosted in their original packages. These should be pierced or slit and any metal ties should be removed and replaced by string or an elastic band.

16 Cakes, bread and bread products, buns, scones, biscuits and pastry items should be placed on absorbent kitchen paper, plain white paper towels or napkins to absorb moisture.

17 Vegetables are best cooked directly from the freezer without being defrosted.

18 If large items of food begin to thaw unevenly, small pieces of smooth aluminium foil may be used to cover any areas which appear to be developing hot spots or beginning to cook.

19 Remember the defrosting process will continue during the standing time. Do not attempt to completely defrost foods in a microwave oven, otherwise the outer edges will dry out, or even begin to cook.

DEFROSTING GUIDE				
Food	No. of items	Weight or size	Approximate time on LOW setting	Further instructions
BREAD				
loaf, whole	1	large	6–8 minutes	Uncover and place in cooker on paper towel. Turn over during defrosting. Stand for 5–15 minutes.
loaf, whole	1	small	4–6 minutes	
loaf, sliced	1	large	6–8 minutes	Defrost in original wrapper but remove any metal tags. Stand for 10–15 minutes.
loaf, sliced	1	small	4–6 minutes	
slice of bread	1	25-g (1-oz)	10–15 seconds	Place on paper towel. Time carefully. Stand for 1–2 minutes.
bread rolls	2	—	15–20 seconds	Place on paper towel. Time carefully. Stand for 2–3 minutes.
	4	—	25–35 seconds	
crumpets	2	—	15–20 seconds	As above
CAKES				
cakes	2	small	30–60 seconds	Place on paper towel. Stand for 5 minutes.
	4	small	1–1½ minutes	
sponge cake	1	450-g (1-lb)	1–1½ minutes	Place on paper towel. Test and turn after 1 minute. Stand for 5 minutes.
cream sponge	1	15-cm (6-in) diameter	30 seconds on HIGH	Place on paper towel. Stand for 20–30 minutes.
jam doughnuts	2	—	45–60 seconds	Place on paper towel. Do not eat immediately as the jam will be very hot. Stand for 5 minutes.
	4	—	45–90 seconds	
cream doughnuts	2	—	45–60 seconds	Place on paper towel. Check after half the defrosting time. Stand for 10 minutes.
	4	—	1¼–1¾ minutes	
cream éclairs	2	—	45 seconds	Stand for 5–10 minutes.
	4	—	1–1½ minutes	Stand for 15–20 minutes.
choux buns	4	small	1–1½ minutes	Stand for 20–30 minutes.
DAIRY PRODUCTS				
butter or margarine	1 pack	250-g (8.82-oz)	1½–2 minutes	Remove foil wrapping if necessary and place block on paper towel. Stand for 5 minutes.
cream, whipped		300 ml (½ pint)	1–2 minutes	Remove metal lid if necessary. Stand for 10–15 minutes.
cream cheese		75 g (3 oz)	1–1½ minutes	Remove foil wrapping. Place on paper towel. Stand for 10–15 minutes.

DEFROSTING GUIDE (contd)

Food	No. of items	Weight or size	Approximate time on LOW setting	Further instructions
DESSERTS				
cheesecake with fruit topping	1	about 23-cm (9-in) diameter	3–4 minutes	Place on serving dish. Stand for 20 minutes.
fruit pie	1	650-g (26-oz)	4–5 minutes	Stand for 5–10 minutes.
mousse	1	individual	30 seconds	Remove lid before defrosting. Stand for 15–20 minutes.
trifles and melbas	1	individual	45–60 seconds	Remove lid before defrosting. Stand for 15–20 minutes.
FISH				
white fish fillets or cutlets, eg cod, coley, haddock, halibut, or whole plaice or sole		450 g (1 lb)	3–4 minutes plus 2–3 minutes	Stand for 5 minutes between defrosts and for 5 minutes afterwards.
oily fish, eg mackerel, herring, trout, whole and gutted		225 g (8 oz)	2–3 minutes plus 3–4 minutes	Stand for 5 minutes between defrosts and for 5 minutes afterwards.
kipper fillets		225 g (8 oz)	2–3 minutes	
lobster tails		225 g (8 oz)	3–4 minutes plus 2–3 minutes	Stand for 5 minutes between defrosts and for 5 minutes afterwards.
prawns, shrimps, scampi, crabmeat	1 block	450-g (1-lb)	2–3 minutes plus 2–3 minutes	Stand for 5 minutes between defrosts and for 5 minutes afterwards.
prawns		100 g (4 oz)	2½ minutes	Pierce plastic bag if necessary. Stand for 2 minutes. Stir. Separate with a fork after 2 minutes. Stand for 3 minutes, then plunge into cold water and drain.
prawns		225 g (8 oz)	3–4 minutes	
FRUIT				
soft fruit, eg strawberries, raspberries		225 g (8 oz)	3–5 minutes	Leave to stand until completely thawed. Stir gently during defrosting and standing time.
		450 g (1 lb)	6–8 minutes	
fruit juice concentrate	1 can	178-ml (6¼-oz)	2–3 minutes	Remove the collar and lid. Stand for 3–5 minutes.

MEAT

Meats may be defrosted in their original paper wrapping, but remember to place even wrapped meat in a shallow dish to catch the juices as the meat thaws. Large joints require 'rest' periods during defrosting to prevent meat starting to cook on the outside before the centre has thawed.

Beef

Food	No. of items	Weight or size	Approximate time on LOW setting	Further instructions
roasting joints, eg sirloin, topside		per 450 g (1 lb)	8–10 minutes	Turn over regularly during defrosting and rest if the meat shows signs of cooking. Stand for 1 hour.
joints on bone, eg rib of beef		per 450 g (1 lb)	10–12 minutes	Cover bone end with foil. Turn joint over during defrosting. The meat will still be icy in the centre but will complete thawing if you stand for 1 hour.

DEFROSTING GUIDE (contd)

Food	No. of items	Weight or size	Approximate time on LOW setting	Further instructions
MEAT: Beef (contd)				
minced beef		450 g (1 lb)	8–10 minutes	Stand for 10 minutes.
cubed steak		450 g (1 lb)	6–8 minutes	Stand for 10 minutes.
steak, eg sirloin, rump		per 450 g (1 lb)	8–10 minutes	Stand for 10 minutes.
beefburgers standard	2 4	50-g (2-oz)	2 minutes 2–3 minutes	Can be cooked from frozen, without defrosting first, if preferred.
quarter-pounder	2 4	100-g (4-oz)	2–3 minutes 5 minutes	
burger buns	2		2 minutes	Stand for 2 minutes.
Lamb/Veal joints		per 450 g (1 lb)	5–6 minutes	Cover any narrow ends, eg leg of lamb, with foil. Turn over during defrosting. Stand for 30–45 minutes.
lamb spare ribs		450 g (1 lb)	6–8 minutes	Stand for 10 minutes.
minced lamb or veal		450 g (1 lb)	8–10 minutes	Stand for 10 minutes.
lamb chops		450 g (1 lb)	8–10 minutes	Separate during defrosting. Stand for 10 minutes
Pork joints		per 450 g (1 lb)	7–8 minutes	Cover narrow or bone ends with foil. Turn over during defrosting. Stand for 1 hour.
fillet or tenderloin		450 g (1 lb)	8–10 minutes	Stand for 10 minutes.
chops		450 g (1 lb)	8–10 minutes	Separate during defrosting and arrange 'spoke' fashion. Stand for 10 minutes.
sausages		450 g (1 lb)	5–6 minutes	Separate during defrosting. Stand for 10 minutes.
Offal liver		450 g (1 lb)	8–10 minutes	If sliced, separate during defrosting. Stand for 5 minutes.
kidney		450 g (1 lb)	6–9 minutes	Separate during defrosting. Stand for 5 minutes.
Bacon rashers	1 pack	225-g (8-oz)	2 minutes	Remove slices from pack and separate after defrosting. Stand for 6–8 minutes.
PASTRY shortcrust and puff	1 pack	227-g (8-oz)	1 minute	Stand for 20 minutes.
	1 pack	395-g (14-oz)	2 minutes	Stand for 20–30 minutes.

DEFROSTING GUIDE (contd)				
Food	No. of items	Weight or size	Approximate time on LOW setting	Further instructions
POULTRY whole chicken or duckling	1	per 450 g (1 lb)	6–8 minutes	Stand in cold water for 30 minutes. Remove giblets.
whole turkey	1	per 450 g (1 lb)	1 minute plus 30 seconds	First minute, breast side up. Rest for 30 minutes then defrost 30 seconds breast side down. Stand in cold water for 2–3 hours. Remove giblets.
chicken portions		450 g (1 lb)	5–7 minutes	Separate during defrosting. Stand for 10 minutes.
RICE cooked		225 g (8 oz)	2 minutes	Break up with a fork after 1 minute.
VEGETABLES As these can be cooked from frozen, refer to the cooking chart on pages 76–78.				

Reheating Food

The majority of foods can be reheated in a microwave oven without loss of quality, colour or flavour. Some, such as meat casseroles using the cheaper cuts of meat, benefit from being cooked on one day, refrigerated overnight after cooling and reheated gently the following day. This helps to tenderise the meat and improve the flavour.

Reheating Guidelines

1 Main course and meat dishes benefit from more gentle heating on low rather than high settings, especially if they have been refrigerated. Cover tightly during reheating.
2 Stir casseroles and main dishes if possible during reheating, to distribute heat and shorten the reheating period.
3 Dishes which cannot be stirred should be rotated manually at appropriate intervals in the ovens of models without turntables.
4 Thin slices of meat will heat more evenly than thickly cut slices. Add sauce or gravy to provide moisture and prevent the meat from drying during reheating.
5 If you want to serve food on to a plate to reheat later, arrange it in an even layer, placing dense foods towards the outside of the plate and quicker heating foods in the centre. Cover plate with cling film to retain heat and moisture.
6 Vegetables in sauce reheat well in a covered dish. They should

be stirred during reheating if possible, otherwise rotate the dish, especially in ovens without a turntable.

7 Care is needed when reheating some vegetables without sauce, to prevent overcooking. Fibrous vegetables such as broccoli spears and asparagus tend to lose texture and toughen when reheated.

8 Wrap bread and bread products in kitchen paper towel to absorb moisture and do not overheat, otherwise they will toughen. One bread roll will be warm in about 10 seconds, and two will only need 10 to 15 seconds.

9 Cooked pastry items should be placed on kitchen paper towel to absorb moisture during reheating. Remember such foods heat extremely quickly in a microwave oven, especially if they have a sweet filling, eg fruit pies. The outer pastry will feel barely warm, but the filling will be very hot—the heat will equalise during a few minutes standing time. One mince pie will be heated in about 10 seconds. The oven should *not* be left unattended during these short reheating periods.

10 Rice and pasta reheat beautifully. The dish should be tightly covered with cling film, and the contents stirred during the reheating period.

11 Exercise care when reheating starchy vegetables such as jacket potatoes to prevent overcooking or dehydration. Wrapping in cling film helps to retain moisture.

12 Test for readiness when reheating food by feeling the bottom of the dish or plate, especially in the centre. If the food is hot enough it will have transferred some heat to the plate or dish.

13 Refrigerated and frozen food will take longer to reheat than food at room temperature, frozen food requiring the longest time.

14 It is often an advantage to undercook food initially if reheating is planned.

Glossary of Terms

Arcing
Small sparks in the oven during cooking. This may occur if metallic foil covering food touches the metal oven lining or if the lining itself is scratched through careless cleaning.
Arcing can damage the magnetron.

Cavity
The term used to describe the inside of the oven.

Electro-magnetic waves
Converted electrical energy used also in radio, television, radar and long distance telephone calls.

Food-sensor
A special type of thermometer which is inserted into the centre of foods and connected to a plug on the inside of the oven. It automatically senses the temperature of the food and reduces the power setting of the oven once the pre-selected temperature has been reached. Also called a temperature probe.

Magnetron
The tube which converts electrical energy into electro-magnetic waves.
Similar to the tubes used for television.

Microwaves
High frequency or very short electro-magnetic waves.

Standing time
The time food needs to complete cooking after it has been taken out of the oven.

Stirrer
A type of fan blade fitted in the top of some microwave ovens for distributing the microwaves to different parts of the oven to assist in the even cooking of food.
They stir the air not the food.

Turntable or rotating platform
Fitted in some microwave ovens for the purpose of turning the food round so it will cook evenly.

Variable power
The ability to vary the amount of power used by the cooker thus controlling the speed of cooking and heating.

Wattage input/output
The highest wattage marked on the cooker is the input of power. Some of this is used to convert the electrical energy into microwaves. The lowest wattage figure marked on the cooker is the output of power which is used for cooking and heating food.
The higher the wattage output the speedier the cooking will be.

RECIPES

All recipes in this book have been tested in countertop portable microwave ovens with a power output rating of between 600–700 watts with and without a built-in turntable. All cooking times given are approximate, and intended as a guide only, since they will be affected by various factors such as starting temperature, density, thickness and quality of the food, as well as the size, type and shape of dish used and of course personal taste. Times will also vary depending on the actual cooking performance of each individual model. Always underestimate cooking time and test food for readiness, to prevent overcooking. Refer to the manufacturer's instruction manual for specific times for your particular oven.

When food is covered, this is stated in the recipe. If no cover is mentioned, leave uncovered.

Servings

Most recipes will serve four people, unless otherwise stated. It is advisable initially to use the exact quantities given in each recipe, since any alteration to quantities will affect the times given.

Measuring the Ingredients

Recipe ingredients are given in Metric and Imperial measurements. The figures are not exact conversions but convenient equivalents. Use either the Metric or Imperial measurements in a recipe, but do not mix the two.

Variable Power Output

Only two microwave oven settings are used, and they represent the power output levels most commonly found, by whatever name or number, on most models.

Setting	Approx. Percentage of Microwave Energy	Approx. Wattage
HIGH	100	600–700
LOW	30–50	200–300

The HIGH setting is used to cook most foods in the recipes in this book. The LOW setting is used to defrost food and to cook some foods which benefit from a longer slower cooking period.

Lower Output Ovens   Ovens with a lower power output will require additional time in the following approximate amounts.

600–700 Watts	500–600 Watts	400–500 Watts
15 secs	17.5 secs	20.5 secs
30 secs	34.5 secs	40.5 secs
1 min	1 min 9 secs	1 min 21 secs
2 mins	2 mins 22 secs	2 mins 42 secs
4 mins	4 mins 36 secs	5 mins 24 secs
5 mins	5 mins 45 secs	6 mins 45 secs
10 mins	11 mins 30 secs	13 mins 30 secs
15 mins	17 mins 15 secs	20 mins 15 secs
20 mins	23 mins	27 mins
25 mins	25 mins 45 secs	33 mins 45 secs
30 mins	34 mins 30 secs	40 mins 30 secs

Always underestimate the times required to defrost, heat or cook food, watch the food as it cooks in the oven, test frequently for readiness; and remember that food will continue to cook by heat conduction after it is removed from the oven, during standing.

Hot Drinks

Making hot drinks in a microwave oven is easy and quick. They can also be made, in most cases, in the cup from which they are to be drunk or the container from which they are served.

If heating more than two cups or mugs at a time, they should be arranged in a ring with space between them, leaving the centre empty. Always stir liquids before placing them to heat in the oven. This is to avoid any surface tension resulting from heating liquid under a skin causing a minor eruption! Remember to leave a space between the surface of the liquid and the brim of the cup or container to avoid any spillage as the liquid expands. Watch drinks heat through the oven door, especially when heating milk-based liquids which can boil over. As boiling starts, simply open the oven door, to prevent spillage. Add instant coffee, tea or Bovril after heating the appropriate liquid, to avoid a bitter taste.

Microwave ovens are ideal for reheating leftover percolated coffee, or that forgotten half cup of tea or coffee which has gone cold.

HOT DRINKS CHART

Beverage	Amount	Approx. Time on High
Milk or water for instant coffee, tea, cocoa or Bovril	1 cup or mug 2 cups or mugs 4 cups or mugs	$1\frac{3}{4}$–$2\frac{3}{4}$ minutes 3 –$4\frac{3}{4}$ minutes 5 –$8\frac{1}{2}$ minutes
Reheating coffee, tea or cocoa made with milk or water	1 cup or mug 2 cups or mugs 4 cups or mugs	$1\frac{1}{2}$–$2\frac{1}{2}$ minutes 2 –$3\frac{1}{2}$ minutes 4 –$6\frac{1}{2}$ minutes

1 cup = 175 ml (6 fl oz)   1 mug = 225 ml (8 fl oz)

When heating more than one mug of liquid place the cups or mugs in a circle with space between them and in the centre. Leave sufficient space at the top for the liquid to expand. Milk-based drinks should be watched carefully.

Mulled Cider

1 litre (1¾ pints) apple cider
45 ml (3 level tbsp) brown
   sugar
pinch of ground nutmeg
6 cloves
1 cinnamon stick
1 orange, sliced

1 Place the cider, sugar and nutmeg in a large bowl.
2 Tie the cloves and cinnamon stick in a small square of cheesecloth or muslin and drop into the cider.
3 Microwave on HIGH for 4–5 minutes or until hot, stirring once or twice during heating.
4 Leave to stand for 5 minutes.
5 Remove the spice bag and serve hot in punch or heatproof glasses, decorated with orange slices.

SERVES 4

Dubonnet Punch

½ bottle red Dubonnet
15 ml (1 tbsp) lemon juice
15 ml (1 level tbsp) brown sugar
400 ml (¾ pint) unsweetened
   orange juice
30 ml (2 tbsp) dark rum
orange and lemon slices, cut in
   half

1 Place all the ingredients except the fruit slices in a large bowl and stir well.
2 Microwave on HIGH for 7–8 minutes, or until hot, stirring once or twice during heating.
3 Serve hot in punch or heatproof glasses, decorated with the orange and lemon slices.

SERVES 4–6

A microwave oven is ideal for making small quantities of punch or hot mulled drinks. Heatproof glass bowls and glasses are ideal serving containers.

Vegetables: from top to bottom, Cauliflower Cheese (page 80) and a selection of cooked fresh vegetables (pages 82–84).

Rice and Pasta

Both rice and pasta take almost as long to cook in a micro-wave oven as they do by conventional methods of cooking. This is because they need to rehydrate first. So, although the method for cooking them is given in the chart below, your microwave may be used to greater advantage by cooking the sauce in the microwave oven while you cook the rice or pasta in the normal way. Both respond to being reheated as they do not lose their *al dente* texture.

Do remember to use a large non-metallic container for cooking purposes as both rice and pasta increase by about three times their dry volume. It is advisable to consult the manufacturer's instructions of each oven before covering. Where this is recommended it should still be sufficiently loose for steam to escape. In both cases the standing time of about 10 minutes is important for the completion of the cooking process.

When reheating pasta, whether it has been refrigerated or not, it should be placed in a lightly covered, non-metallic container and cooked until it starts to steam. Stir it at least once during this time. The same is true of rice which may also be reheated straight from the freezer.

RICE AND PASTA COOKING CHART

Food	Amount	Preparation	Approximate Cooking Time on High	Further Instructions
Long grain rice	225 g (8 oz)	Place in a deep 2.5-litre (4½-pint) covered bowl with 600 ml (1 pint) boiling salted water and 15 ml (1 tbsp) vegetable oil.	10–12 minutes	Leave to stand covered for 10 minutes after removing from oven.
Macaroni, small pasta, noodles	225 g (8 oz)	Place in a deep 2.5-litre (4½-pint) covered bowl with 600 ml (1 pint) boiling salted water and 15 ml (1 tbsp) vegetable oil.	10–15 minutes	Leave to stand covered for 10 minutes after removing from oven.
Spaghetti	225 g (8 oz)	Hold spaghetti in 1 litre (1¾ pints) boiling salted water in a 2.5-litre (4½-pint) bowl to submerge as it softens. Add 15 ml (1 tbsp) vegetable oil and cover bowl.	10–15 minutes	Leave to stand covered for 10–15 minutes after removing from oven.

Light meals: from the top left, clockwise, Tomato and Yogurt Soup Cups (*page 75*), Welsh Rarebit (*page 72*) and a Cheeseburger (*page 72*).

Snacks

The microwave is ideal for preparing snacks for the family at any time of the day. They are quick to prepare and simple enough for even the younger members of the family to follow.

Baked Beans or Spaghetti on Toast

1 slice toasted bread, buttered
45 ml (3 tbsp) canned baked beans or spaghetti in tomato sauce

1 Place the hot toast on a suitable serving plate.
2 Spoon the beans or spaghetti on to the toast.
3 Microwave on HIGH for 1–1½ minutes and serve immediately.

SERVES 1

Note Beans may 'pop' during the heating period. Do not overheat.

Cheeseburgers

ILLUSTRATED ON PAGE 70

4 × 50-g (2-oz) beefburgers
4 baps, split and buttered
4 processed cheese slices
20 ml (4 tsp) tomato ketchup

1 Place the beefburgers in a circle on a piece of absorbent kitchen paper on a plate.
2 Microwave on HIGH for 1½–2 minutes.
3 Turn over the beefburgers and microwave on HIGH for a further 1–1½ minutes.
4 Place in the buttered baps and top with the cheese slices and tomato ketchup.
5 Replace the filled baps in a circle on the kitchen paper and microwave on HIGH for 1–1½ minutes. Do not overheat or the baps will toughen.
6 Leave to stand for 1 minute before serving.

SERVES 4

Welsh Rarebit

ILLUSTRATED ON PAGE 70

25 g (1 oz) butter
5 ml (1 level tsp) dry mustard
pinch of salt
pinch of cayenne pepper
dash of Worcestershire sauce
75 g (3 oz) mature Cheddar cheese, grated
30 ml (2 tbsp) brown ale
2 slices toasted bread

1 Place the butter in a medium-sized bowl and microwave on HIGH for 20 seconds to soften.
2 Add the mustard, seasoning, Worcestershire sauce, grated cheese and ale and mix well.
3 Microwave on HIGH for about 30 seconds.
4 Beat well and spread over the toast. Place on appropriate serving plates.
5 Microwave on HIGH for 20–30 seconds and serve immediately.

SERVES 2

Cheese and Tomato Open Sandwich

1 slice toasted bread,
 preferably wholemeal or rye
mayonnaise
lettuce
tomato slices
1 Cheddar or processed cheese
 slice

1 Spread the toasted bread with mayonnaise and cover with lettuce.
2 Place tomato slices on the lettuce and top with the cheese.
3 Arrange on a white paper napkin on a plate.
4 Microwave on HIGH for 15–30 seconds. Do not overheat.

SERVES 1

Note Watch the sandwich heat through the oven door. Times vary with the amount of topping and those topped with cheese heat very very quickly.

Bacon Sandwich

2 slices streaky bacon, rind
 removed
2 slices bread

1 Snip the bacon fat at intervals to prevent curling.
2 Place the bacon slices on a suitable plate and cover with absorbent kitchen paper.
3 Microwave on HIGH for $1\frac{1}{2}$–2 minutes, depending on the thickness of the bacon.
4 Sandwich the bacon between the slices of bread which have been dipped in the melted bacon fat.
5 Place the sandwich on a serving plate and cover with cling film.
6 Microwave on HIGH for about 30 seconds. Do not overheat.
7 Remove the cling film, cut in half and serve.

SERVES 1

Placing absorbent kitchen paper over bacon while it is cooking in a microwave oven, allows steam to escape while preventing fat from spattering the walls of the oven.

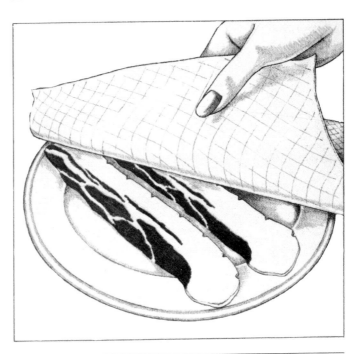

Soups

Homemade soups can be prepared with speed, either to serve immediately or to refrigerate and reheat as required. Make speedy stock for soups by microwaving bones, seasonings and water for 20 minutes on HIGH, followed by 20 minutes standing time. Cook them in the serving dish or tureen from which you intend to serve them. Always choose a container larger than the amount being cooked, to prevent spillage.

For even quicker results, use your microwave to heat canned and dehydrated soups. Canned soups can be heated in individual soup bowls, or even mugs, for family snacks. Dehydrated soup mixes are best left to stand in the recommended amount of water for about 30 minutes to soften before heating.

How to Heat Canned Soup

1 Pour the soup into a large jug, individual soup bowls or a soup tureen, diluting if recommended by the manufacturer, eg condensed soups.
2 Cover with a piece of cling film.
3 Microwave on HIGH until hot. A 435-g (15-oz) can will require 3–4 minutes.
4 Stir the soup after removing from the oven.
5 Leave to stand, covered, for a few minutes before serving.

Note Mushroom and cream soups are best heated more slowly on the LOW setting and will, therefore, require a longer heating time.

How to Cook Dehydrated Soup Mixes

1 Reconstitute according to the packet instructions in a large ovenproof jug or bowl which should be no more than two thirds full.
2 Allow to soak for about 30 minutes to soften.
3 Cover with cling film.
4 Microwave on HIGH to bring to the boil, eg 600–750 ml (1–1$\frac{1}{4}$ pints) 6–8 minutes; 1 litre (1$\frac{3}{4}$ pints) 8–10 minutes.
5 Stir and leave to stand, covered, for a few minutes before serving.

Note Soup mixes containing dehydrated rice or noodles should be soaked as above before bringing to the boil on HIGH and continuing to cook on LOW until the rice or noodles are tender.

French Onion Soup

50 g (2 oz) butter
550 g (1¼ lb) onions, thinly sliced
4 beef stock cubes
salt and pepper
75 g (3 oz) Gruyère cheese, grated
4–6 toasted rounds of French bread

1 Place the butter in a large bowl or tureen and microwave on HIGH for 30 seconds until melted. Stir in the onion slices to coat with the butter.
2 Cover with cling film and microwave on HIGH for 8 minutes.
3 Dissolve the stock cubes in 1 litre (1¾ pints) boiling water. Stir into the onions and re-cover.
4 Microwave on HIGH for about 15 minutes, stirring once during cooking.
5 Leave the soup to stand, covered.
6 Meanwhile, divide the cheese between the toasted French bread.
7 Arrange the bread in a circle on a suitable plate and microwave on HIGH for 1–1½ minutes to melt the cheese.
8 Uncover the soup, float the toast on top and serve immediately.

SERVES 4–6

Cream of Mushroom Soup

50 g (2 oz) butter
1 small onion, chopped
2 chicken stock cubes
225 g (8 oz) button mushrooms sliced
bouquet garni
25 g (1 oz) cornflour
300 ml (½ pint) milk
salt and pepper
50 ml (2 fl oz) single cream

1 Place the butter and chopped onion in a large 2.5-litre (4½-pint) bowl or casserole. Cover with cling film.
2 Microwave on HIGH for 4–5 minutes.
3 Dissolve the stock cubes in 600 ml (1 pint) boiling water and add to the onion with the sliced mushrooms and bouquet garni. Re-cover and microwave on HIGH for 15–20 minutes.
4 Remove the bouquet garni and either sieve or liquidise the soup.
5 Blend the cornflour to a cream with a little of the measured milk, then stir in the remaining milk.
6 Add to the mushroom mixture and re-cover.
7 Microwave on HIGH for about 10 minutes, stirring once.
8 Season to taste, pour into a serving dish and swirl the cream on top.

SERVES 4–6

Tomato and Yogurt Soup Cups

ILLUSTRATED ON PAGE 70

298-g (10½-oz) can condensed tomato soup, diluted according to instructions
15 ml (1 tbsp) lemon juice
15 ml (1 tbsp) caster sugar
2 medium tomatoes, skinned and chopped
60 ml (4 tbsp) natural yogurt
60 ml (4 level tbsp) chopped chives

1 Combine the diluted soup, lemon juice and sugar.
2 Divide the tomatoes between three to four soup cups.
3 Add the soup and cover each cup with cling film.
4 Place the cups in a circle in the oven.
5 Microwave on HIGH for 6–8 minutes or until the soup just comes to the boil.
6 Carefully remove the hot soup cups.
7 Pierce the cling film before removing it from the cups.
8 Swirl a tablespoon of yogurt on the top of each cup of soup, sprinkle with chives and serve immediately.

SERVES 3–4

Appetisers

An appetiser makes an occasion of a meal, and adds something special to party food. The advantage of using a microwave oven to cook them in is that it gives the host or hostess more time to spend welcoming the guests rather than over the stove.

Walnut Spread or Dip

200-g (8-oz) packet cream cheese
150-ml (5-fl oz) carton natural yogurt
15 ml (1 tbsp) melted butter
45 ml (3 level tbsp) chopped green pepper
15 ml (1 level tbsp) chopped red pepper
5 ml (1 level tsp) garlic salt
pinch of black pepper
100 g (4 oz) walnuts, chopped
paprika

1 Place the cream cheese in an ovenproof glass bowl and microwave on HIGH for 30–45 seconds to soften. Add the yogurt and butter and beat well until smooth.
2 Stir in the green and red pepper, garlic salt, black pepper and most of the walnuts and mix well.
3 Turn the mixture into a serving dish and refrigerate until cold and thickened.
4 Sprinkle with paprika and remaining walnuts.
5 Either serve the spread on small savoury biscuits or as a dip, accompanied by raw vegetables, such as carrot sticks, cauliflower florets and radishes, and Melba toast.

SERVES ABOUT 12

Bacon Wands

12 slices streaky bacon, rind removed
12 gris sticks or breadsticks

1 Wrap each slice of bacon, spiral fashion, round a gris stick.
2 Place 6 at a time on absorbent kitchen paper on a suitable plate. Arrange them so that they are evenly spaced on the plate and not too close together.
3 Cover loosely with absorbent kitchen paper.
4 Microwave on HIGH for 2–3 minutes, turn each one over and microwave on HIGH for about a further 3 minutes, or until the bacon is crisp.
5 Serve immediately.

MAKES 12

Bacon wands are an ideal appetiser as they can be made in advance of when they are needed and still stay crisp. Wind each bacon strip diagonally around a gris or breadstick and place on a plate or microwave baking tray.

Stuffed Bacon Appetisers

6 slices streaky bacon, rind removed
18 large stuffed olives

1 Cut each slice of bacon into three pieces.
2 Wrap the olives in bacon and secure with wooden cocktail sticks.
3 Arrange on absorbent kitchen paper on a suitably large plate to allow spaces in between.
4 Cover loosely with absorbent kitchen paper.
5 Microwave on HIGH for 2–3 minutes, turn each roll over and microwave on HIGH for a further 3 minutes or until the bacon is crisp.
6 Serve immediately.

MAKES 18

Variations Replace the olives with 18 cooked stoned prunes or 18 large cooked and peeled shrimps or prawns and proceed as above.

Kipper Pâté

225 g (8 oz) frozen kipper fillets
75 g (3 oz) butter
30 ml (2 tbsp) single cream
anchovy essence to taste
salt and pepper

1 Place the kippers, in original wrapping on a plate. Cut a cross in the wrapping with a pair of scissors.
2 Microwave on LOW for about 8 minutes to defrost.
3 Place the butter in a small glass bowl and microwave on HIGH for 45–60 seconds or until melted.
4 Place the kippers in a blender or food processor with the cream, anchovy essence, seasoning and two thirds of the butter. Blend until smooth, turn off and scrape down the sides of the goblet from time to time.
5 Turn the pâté into a small dish or individual ramekins and top with the remaining melted butter.
6 Refrigerate.
7 Serve with hot buttered toast.

SERVES 3–4

Pigs in Blankets

4 processed cheese slices
mustard or pickle
4 frankfurters
4 slices streaky bacon, rind removed

1 Spread the cheese slices with mustard or pickle and wrap round the frankfurters.
2 Wrap the bacon round the cheese.
3 Arrange in a circle on absorbent kitchen paper on a large plate or flat dish.
4 Cover loosely with absorbent kitchen paper and microwave on HIGH for 4–5 minutes or until the frankfurters are warm and the bacon is crisp. Turn the frankfurters over after 2 minutes.
5 Remove kitchen paper immediately and serve.

SERVES 4

Eggs and Cheese

Both eggs and cheese take a remarkably short time to cook, which makes them ideal for last-minute dishes. But because of this very speed, care must be taken not to overcook them as they will toughen equally quickly. Cooking times are given as a guide only, since personal tastes vary, but remember that both eggs and cheese will continue to cook for a short while after their removal from the oven, so it is advisable to undercook slightly.

In particular, eggs in their shells should never be cooked, or reheated if previously hard-boiled. Ideally, eggs should be at room temperature prior to cooking. They should be broken on to a plate or into a dish and the yolks pricked with a cocktail stick or sharp pointed knife, otherwise they may burst. Processed cheese melts more smoothly than natural cheese and very finely grated cheese cuts down on the stirring needed. If you remember these guidelines you should always be successful.

Alpine Fondue

1 garlic clove, crushed
300 ml ($\frac{1}{2}$ pint) dry white wine
25 g (1 oz) cornflour
225 g (8 oz) Gruyère cheese,
grated
225 g (8 oz) Emmenthal cheese,
grated
pepper
30 ml (2 tbsp) kirsch
cubes of French bread to serve

1 Rub the crushed garlic round the inside of a 1.5-litre (2$\frac{1}{2}$-pint) ovenproof glass bowl or non-metallic fondue pot.
2 Add the wine, cover and microwave on LOW for 8–10 minutes.
3 Mix the cornflour with the grated cheese and gradually stir into the heated wine until combined. Add the pepper.
4 Microwave on LOW for about 6 minutes or until the cheese has melted, stirring every minute.
5 Stir in the kirsch and, if necessary, return to the oven to heat on LOW for 1–2 minutes.
6 Serve with cubes of French bread, keeping the fondue warm over a spirit burner if possible. If not, the fondue can be returned to the microwave oven to reheat, if required.

SERVES 4–6

Cheese dishes, like a fondue, only take minutes to reach the table. Stir the cheese and cornflour into the heated wine in a heatproof pottery fondue dish and complete the recipe. When the fondue is ready, each person should spear a cube of bread on a long fondue fork and dip it into the fondue.

Cheese Pudding

3 eggs, beaten
568 ml (1 pint) milk
pinch of dry mustard
salt and pepper
225 g (8 oz) brown
    breadcrumbs
175 g (6 oz) mature Cheddar
    cheese, grated

1 Mix together the beaten eggs, milk, mustard and seasoning.
2 Pour the mixture over the breadcrumbs and cheese and mix well.
3 Turn into a buttered 1.25-litre (2-pint) round dish and cover with cling film.
4 Microwave on LOW for about 15 minutes or until just set, rotating the dish every 5 minutes in models without a turntable.
5 Leave to stand, covered, for 5 minutes.
6 Test for readiness by inserting a knife in the centre. If it comes out clean, the pudding is set and ready to serve.

SERVES 4

Variation Sprinkle an additional 50 g (2 oz) of grated cheese over the top and brown under a preheated grill.

Egg and Bacon

2 slices streaky bacon, rind
    removed
1 egg

1 Snip the bacon fat at intervals to prevent curling.
2 Place the bacon slices on a serving plate or in a shallow dish and cover with absorbent kitchen paper.
3 Microwave on HIGH for 1–1½ minutes depending on the thickness of the bacon.
4 Remove from the plate or dish and add the egg.
5 Prick the egg yolk and cover with cling film.
6 Microwave on HIGH for about 30 seconds and leave to stand for 1 minute.
7 Return the bacon to the plate or dish and cook, covered, for 15–30 seconds.

SERVES 1

ILLUSTRATED ON PAGE 18

Scrambled Eggs

No. of Eggs	Milk	Butter (Optional)	Approx. Time on HIGH
2	30 ml (2 tbsp)	15 g (½ oz)	1½–2 minutes
4	60 ml (4 tbsp)	25 g (1 oz)	2–2½ minutes

1 Beat the eggs and milk together in a glass measuring jug or bowl.
2 Add the butter, if used, season to taste and stir to mix.
3 Microwave on HIGH for the required time, stirring every 30 seconds.
4 Cook until they are still soft in the centre as they will continue to cook during the 1–2 minutes standing time.
5 Stir with a fork before serving on hot buttered toast.

Poached Eggs

400 ml (¾ pint) boiling salted
  water
2.5 ml (½ tsp) white vinegar
2 eggs

1 Put the water and vinegar into a large shallow ovenproof dish and microwave on HIGH for 1–2 minutes or until the water comes back to the boil.

2 Carefully break each egg on to a saucer, prick the yolk and slide one at a time into the water.

3 Cover the dish with cling film and microwave on HIGH for about 1 minute.

4 Pierce the cling film and leave the eggs to stand, covered, for 1–2 minutes to set. Using a slotted spoon, transfer the eggs on to hot buttered toast.

SERVES 2

Note To poach 4 eggs, use 600 ml (1 pint) boiling salted water with 5 ml (1 tsp) vinegar and proceed as above. After adding the eggs, cover and cook for 1½–2 minutes.

ILLUSTRATED ON PAGE 69

Cauliflower Cheese

1 cauliflower, prepared weight
  about 700 g (1½ lb)
60 ml (4 tbsp) water
25 g (1 oz) soft tub margarine
25 g (1 oz) plain flour
300 ml (½ pint) milk
pinch of dry mustard
salt and pepper
75 g (3 oz) cheese, grated

Topping
15 g (½ oz) butter
25 g (1 oz) fresh brown
  breadcrumbs

1 Break the prepared cauliflower into florets and place in a large dish with the water.

2 Cover and microwave on HIGH for 10–12 minutes. Drain.

3 Combine the margarine, flour, milk, mustard and seasoning in a glass measuring jug and blend well together.

4 Microwave on HIGH for about 4 minutes or until the sauce has boiled and thickened, stirring once during cooking.

5 Whisk until smooth, then stir in grated cheese.

6 Pour the sauce over the drained cauliflower in a suitable 1-litre (2-pint) serving dish.

7 For the topping, melt the butter in a dish, then stir in the breadcrumbs. Microwave on HIGH for 2–3 minutes until crisp. Sprinkle on top of the cauliflower.

8 Microwave on HIGH for 3–5 minutes until heated through.

9 Leave to stand for 2–3 minutes before serving.

SERVES 4

Vegetables

Fresh and frozen vegetables cooked in a microwave oven retain their flavour and colour and are crisp yet tender.

Use the following guidelines to achieve perfect results.

1 Only the minimum of water, 30—45 ml (2—3 tbsp), is required for cooking most vegetables, meaning that little goodness is thrown away with the cooking liquid. If you prefer your vegetables softer than the results produced by our charts, add a little more water and extend the cooking time slightly, but be careful not to overcook.

2 Jacket potatoes, courgettes, mushrooms, spinach, corn-on-the-cob and new potatoes only require the water that clings to them from washing.

3 Pierce or prick the skin of whole fresh vegetables such as potatoes or tomatoes before cooking to prevent them bursting.

4 Stir or shake vegetables during cooking, particularly if your oven does not have a turntable.

5 Arrange the stalk ends of vegetables, such as broccoli, towards the outside of the dish, with the heads towards the centre.

6 Season vegetables after cooking as salt sprinkled directly on to vegetables can cause dehydration and toughening.

7 Turn canned vegetables into a suitable non-metallic dish before placing in the oven.

8 If you use roasting bags to cook vegetables in, replace metal ties with string or elastic bands.

9 Prepare vegetables in uniformly sized pieces to ensure even cooking.

Baked potatoes are ideal for cooking in a microwave oven and only take minutes to be ready. Prick each scrubbed potato with a fork in several places. Arrange the potatoes at least 2.5 cm (1 inch) apart in a circle on a piece of absorbent paper. Turn the potatoes over and re-arrange them half way through the cooking time. If you wrap them in aluminium foil they will keep warm for up to 30 minutes.

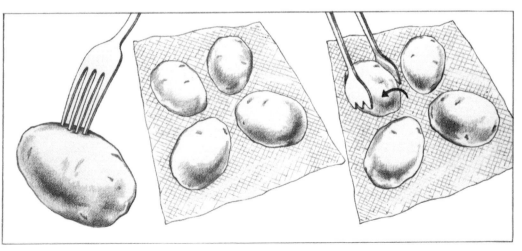

FRESH VEGETABLES COOKING CHART
All times are given as a guide only, since variations in size and quality will affect cooking times.

Vegetables	Preparation	Quantity	Approximate time on HIGH	Further instructions
artichokes, globe	Wash and drain. Cut off stalk at base. Slice off upper tip and trim tips of leaves.	1 2 3	5–6 minutes 7–8 minutes 11–12 minutes	Place upright in covered dish. Serve with mayonnaise, hollandaise, vinaigrette or mornay sauce.
asparagus	Remove white woody part to give even length spears.	350 g (12 oz)	5–7 minutes	Place stalks towards outside of dish. Cooking time may vary with thickness and age. Serve with cheese, lemon, hollandaise or vinaigrette sauce or sour cream.
aubergines	Wash, slice, sprinkle with salt and leave for 30 minutes. Rinse and pat dry.	450 g (1 lb)	8–10 minutes	Stir or shake after 4 minutes.
beans, broad	Shell.	450 g (1 lb)	6–8 minutes	Stir or shake after 3 minutes, and test after 5 minutes.
beans, green	String and slice or leave whole.	450 g (1 lb)	12–16 minutes	Stir or shake during cooking period. Time will vary with age and size.
beetroot—whole, medium	Wash and pierce skin with fork.	4 medium	14–16 minutes	Re-arrange during cooking. Skin and remove stalks after cooking.
broccoli	Wash, remove outer leaves and tough portion of stalk. Slit stem ends to speed up cooking.	450 g (1 lb)	8–10 minutes	Re-arrange during cooking. Serve with cheese, mustard, hollandaise, egg or mornay sauce.
brussels sprouts	Discard outside wilted leaves. Trim and cut a cross in stem stalk end.	225 g (8 oz) 450 g (1 lb)	4–6 minutes 7–10 minutes	Stir or shake during cooking.
cabbage, shredded	Discard damaged and wilted leaves. Trim stalk. Shred.	450 g (1 lb)	9–12 minutes	Stir or shake during cooking.
carrots	Scrape, or peel and slice, or cut into rings.	225 g (8 oz) 450 g (1 lb)	7–8 minutes 10–12 minutes	Stir or shake during cooking.
cauliflower	Trim. Break into florets.	225 g (8 oz) 450 g (1 lb)	7–8 minutes 10–12 minutes	Stir or shake during cooking. Do not sprinkle salt directly on to the vegetable.
celery	Separate sticks and wash. Slice or cut into strips.	350 g (12 oz)	7–10 minutes	Stir or shake during cooking. Serve with cheese sauce.

FRESH VEGETABLES COOKING CHART (contd)

Vegetables	Preparation	Quantity	Approximate time on HIGH	Further instructions
corn-on-the-cob	Remove husk, wash and trim. Wrap individually in greased greaseproof paper. Do *not* add water.	2	6–8 minutes	Turn over after 3 minutes. Serve with melted butter and freshly ground black pepper.
courgettes	Wash, dry and slice. Do not peel. Do not add more than 30 ml (2 tbsp) water.	450 g (1 lb)	12–14 minutes	Stir or shake twice gently during cooking. Stand for 2 minutes before draining.
leeks	Wash very thoroughly, trim and slice.	450 g (1 lb)	8–12 minutes	Stir or shake during cooking.
mushrooms	Trim stalks. Wipe. Do *not* add water. Add 25 g (1 oz) butter and a squeeze of lemon juice.	225 g (8 oz)	2–3 minutes	Time will depend on type, and whether whole or sliced. Stir or shake gently during cooking.
onions	Peel, and slice or leave whole. Do *not* add water.	225 g (8 oz) sliced 175 g (6 oz) whole	4–6 minutes 10–12 minutes	Stir or shake sliced onions and re-arrange whole onions during cooking.
parsnips	Peel, remove hard centre core and cut into quarters or halves depending on size and shape. Place thinner parts towards centre.	450 g (1 lb)	10–12 minutes	Turn dish during cooking and re-arrange.
peas	Shell.	450 g (1 lb)	5–8 minutes	Time will vary with the age of the peas. Stir or shake during cooking.
potatoes **baked jacket**	Wash and prick skin with fork. Place on absorbent kitchen paper or napkin. When cooking more than two at a time, arrange in a circle.	1 175-g (6-oz) potato 2 175-g (6-oz) potatoes 4 175-g (6-oz) potatoes	4 minutes 6–7 minutes 12–14 minutes	Turn over half way through cooking period.
boiled (old)	Wash and peel. Cut into 40 g (1½ oz) pieces.	450 g (1 lb)	7–10 minutes	Stir or shake during cooking period.
boiled (new)	Wash and scrub.	450 g (1 lb)	6–8 minutes	
sweet	Wash and prick skin with fork. Place on absorbent kitchen paper. Use even sized potatoes.	450 g (1 lb)	5 minutes	Turn over half way through cooking period.
spinach	Wash, remove wilted leaves and any tough stems. Do *not* add water.	450 g (1 lb)	6–7 minutes	Turn dish during cooking. Serve with cheese or egg sauce.
swede/turnip	Peel and dice.	450 g (1 lb)	10–15 minutes	Time will vary with age and quality. Stir or shake during cooking. Mash after standing.

FROZEN VEGETABLES COOKING CHART

Frozen vegetables may be cooked straight from the freezer. Many may be cooked in their original plastic packaging or pouch, if it is first slit and placed on a plate or in a dish.

Vegetable	Quantity	Approximate time on HIGH	Further instructions
asparagus	275 g (10 oz)	7–9 minutes	Separate and re-arrange after 3 minutes.
beans, broad	225 g (8 oz)	7–8 minutes	Stir or shake during cooking period.
beans, green cut	225 g (8 oz)	6–8 minutes	Stir or shake during cooking period.
broccoli	275 g (10 oz)	7–9 minutes	Re-arrange spears after 3 minutes.
brussels sprouts	225 g (8 oz)	6–8 minutes	Stir or shake during cooking period.
cauliflower florets	275 g (10 oz)	7–9 minutes	Stir or shake during cooking period.
carrots	225 g (8 oz)	6–7 minutes	Stir or shake during cooking period.
corn-on-the-cob	1 2	3–4 minutes 6–7 minutes	Do not add water. Dot with butter, wrap in greaseproof paper.
mixed vegetables	225 g (8 oz)	5–6 minutes	Stir or shake during cooking period.
peas	225 g (8 oz)	5–6 minutes	Stir or shake during cooking period.
peas and carrots	225 g (8 oz)	7–8 minutes	Stir or shake during cooking period.
spinach, leaf or chopped	275 g (10 oz)	7–9 minutes	Do not add water. Stir or shake during cooking period.
swede/turnip, diced	225 g (8 oz)	6–7 minutes	Stir or shake during cooking period. Mash with butter after standing time.
sweetcorn	225 g (8 oz)	4–6 minutes	Stir or shake during cooking period.

Fish

Whether fresh or frozen, fish correctly cooked in a micro-wave oven is difficult to beat for flavour, texture and appearance. When cooking fish alone, all that is required, in most cases, is the addition of a little butter or lemon juice.

To produce results which are firm but moist always bear the following points in mind:

1 Always cover fish tightly during cooking.

2 Arrange fish so that thicker pieces are towards the outside of the dish and thinner pieces towards the centre.

3 The narrow tail end of whole fish may be covered with small pieces of smooth aluminium foil to prevent over-cooking.

4 Whole fish should have the skin slit in two or three places to prevent bursting.

5 Overcooked fish is dry and tough. Try to avoid the need to reheat fish if there is a possibility that it might overcook.

6 Do not deep fat fry in a microwave oven.

7 Breadcrumbed or battered fish, fish fingers excepted, that is microwaved will produce soggy not crisp results.

8 Boil-in-the-bag fish should have the bag pierced before cooking.

9 Frozen fish can be defrosted on LOW in its original wrapping. Fillets should be separated and whole fish turned over during defrosting. See page 60 for a chart giving times of defrosting for particular sorts of fish.

10 To stop fish drying out, brush with melted butter.

Turbot and Prawn Salad

ILLUSTRATED ON PAGE 87

225 g (8 oz) turbot
100 g (4 oz) peeled prawns
30 ml (2 level tbsp) finely diced green pepper
5 ml (1 tsp) lemon juice
seafood or prawn cocktail sauce
salt and freshly ground black pepper
bunch of watercress or lettuce
black olives
paprika

1 Place the fish on a suitable plate and cover with cling film.

2 Microwave on HIGH for about 3 minutes or until just cooked. If the fish is thick, turn it over after about 1½ minutes.

3 Leave the fish to stand, covered, until cool.

4 Cut the fish into cubes. Add the prawns and green pepper and mix together with the lemon juice and seafood or prawn cocktail sauce.

5 Season to taste.

6 Line 4 scallop shells with watercress or lettuce.

7 Arrange the fish mixture on top and garnish with olives and paprika.

SERVES 4

Variations Use other white fish, such as halibut, cod or haddock, instead of turbot. Replace the prawns with shrimps.

Poached Fish

450 g (1 lb) white fish fillets or
    cutlets
salt and pepper
50 ml (2 fl oz) milk
knob of butter

1 Place the fish in a single layer in a suitable shallow dish.
2 Mix the seasoning with the milk and pour over the fish.
3 Flake the butter on top.
4 Cover the dish tightly with cling film and microwave on HIGH for 5–6 minutes or until the fish is white and flakes when tested with a fork.
5 Leave to stand for about 5 minutes before serving.

SERVES 4

Soused Herrings

4 herrings, cleaned and boned
salt and pepper
150 ml ($\frac{1}{4}$ pint) vinegar
150 ml ($\frac{1}{4}$ pint) water
3–4 peppercorns
1 small onion, sliced

1 Trim the heads, tails and fins from the fish. Remove any remaining bones and sprinkle with salt and pepper.
2 Roll the fish up, skin side out, from the head end. Secure with wooden cocktail sticks.
3 Arrange in a single layer in a suitable shallow dish.
4 Mix the vinegar and water together, add the peppercorns and pour over the fish. Arrange the onion slices on top.
5 Cover and microwave on HIGH for 6–8 minutes, turning the dish after 3 minutes.
6 Leave the fish to cool in the liquid. Chill in the refrigerator before serving with salad.

SERVES 4

ILLUSTRATED OPPOSITE

Salmon Steaks with Hollandaise Sauce

4 salmon steaks, cut 2.5 cm (1
    inch) thick
150 ml ($\frac{1}{4}$ pint) water
15 ml (1 tbsp) lemon juice
2.5 ml ($\frac{1}{2}$ tsp) salt

1 Arrange the steaks in a single layer in a shallow dish with the thickest part of the flesh towards the outside of the dish.
2 Mix the water, lemon juice and salt together and pour over the fish.
3 Cover the dish with cling film and microwave on HIGH for 6–8 minutes or until the water just comes to the boil. Turn the dish twice during cooking if using an oven without a turntable.
4 If serving hot, leave the dish to stand for 5 minutes. If serving cold, leave to cool in the liquid and refrigerate.

SERVES 4

Hollandaise Sauce

125 g (4 oz) butter
30 ml (2 tbsp) lemon juice or
    white wine vinegar
2 egg yolks
salt and pepper

1 Put the butter in a suitable bowl and microwave on HIGH for 1–1$\frac{1}{2}$ minutes until melted.
2 Remove from the oven and whisk in the lemon juice or wine vinegar and egg yolks.
3 Microwave on HIGH for 30–45 seconds or until just thick enough to coat the back of a spoon. Stir briskly after each 15 seconds.
4 Season to taste before serving.

Fish: centre, Salmon Steaks with Hollandaise Sauce
(*above*) surrounded by dishes of Turbot and Prawn
Salad (*page 85*).

Meat

Cooking meat in a microwave oven will reduce cooking times by about one third. As with conventional cooking, the end result will largely depend on the quality of the meat used, but the following guidelines will also be of use:

1 Frozen meat should be completely defrosted before cooking (see page 60).

2 With the exception of roast pork, do not salt meat before cooking as this draws out the moisture and toughens the outside of it.

3 Joints of meat cook more evenly if they are symmetrically shaped—eg boned and rolled.

4 To prevent overcooking of thinner parts cover for half the cooking time with a narrow strip of foil.

5 Shape meat loaf mixtures into individual loaves or cook in a ring mould for faster cooking.

6 When preparing casseroles; first sauté the meat and vegetables separately in the microwave oven using the casserole dish, then combine. No greasy frying pan.

7 Reduce the liquid required for recipes such as casseroles by one third to a half as there is little evaporation with microwave cooking. Vegetables retain their shape, rather than breaking down and thickening the liquid.

8 When preparing stews and casseroles, cut the meat and vegetables into pieces of the same size to ensure even cooking.

9 The tenderness of casseroled meat will increase if the casserole is allowed to cool after cooking and is then reheated when required. Meat casseroles are cooked on LOW to extend the cooking time and allow time for the meat to tenderise and the flavour to develop.

10 Minimise splattering fat by covering sausages, bacon and other fatty meats with paper towels.

11 Use wooden skewers to secure meat.

12 Improve browning of meat by microwaving in a covered glass casserole or pierced roasting bag (fastened with an elastic band). Large joints will brown unassisted because of their longer cooking time.

Meat: from top to bottom, Chilli con Carne (page 92) and Italian Meatballs (page 92).

Meat Roasting Guide

The times given in this chart must only be used as a guide, since there are many variables involved. Follow the oven manufacturer's specific instructions and guidelines for individual models. Place all joints fat side down, either on a microwave roasting rack, or on an upturned saucer in a suitable dish, to raise the meat out of its juices. After half the calculated cooking time, turn the joint fat side up and pour off excess meat juices. Pierced roasting bags can be used to roast meat in the oven. They encourage browning and usually shorten the cooking time slightly.

MEAT ROASTING CHART

Meat	Approximate Cooking Time per 450 g (1 lb) on HIGH	Further Instructions
BEEF Roasting joints off the bone, eg sirloin, topside	Rare—5–6 minutes. Medium—7–8 minutes. Well done—8–10 minutes.	Turn over during cooking. Stand, covered in foil, for 15 minutes.
Joints on bone, eg rib of beef	Rare—5 minutes. Medium—6 minutes. Well done—8 minutes.	Cover bone end with foil during half the cooking period. Stand, covered in foil, for 15 minutes.
LAMB/VEAL Joints	Well done—8–9 minutes.	Cover narrow ends, eg leg of lamb, with foil during half the cooking period. Stand, covered in foil, for 15 minutes.
PORK Joints	Well done—9 minutes.	Cover narrow or bone ends with foil during half the cooking period. Stand, covered in foil, for 15 minutes.

Test joints to see if they are cooked by inserting a meat thermometer in more than one part. Only use special microwave meat thermometers inside the oven. Leave joints to stand for about 15 minutes, covered by a tent of aluminium foil, shiny side in. During this standing time the internal temperature should rise about 5–7°C (10–15°F).

How to Cook Bacon

Cooking bacon requires some extra advice.

1 Snip rind and fat with scissors before cooking, to prevent bacon curling up during cooking.
2 Cook bacon on a special microwave roasting rack or between pieces of absorbent kitchen paper.
3 Always cook in a single layer and pour off excess fat during cooking.
4 Immediately after cooking, remove paper to prevent sticking.

Bacon Slices Cooking Guide

These times are only a guide, as they may vary depending on brand of bacon, starting temperature, thickness, number of slices and personal preference.

No. of Slices	Approximate Time on HIGH
2	2–2½ minutes
4	4–4½ minutes
6	5–6 minutes

Boeuf Bourguignonne

100 g (4 oz) streaky bacon, rinded and chopped
700 g (1½ lb) sirloin steak, cut into 2.5 cm (1 inch) cubes
225 ml (8 fl oz) red wine
1 garlic clove, skinned and chopped
175 g (6 oz) silverskin or baby onions, peeled and left whole
100 g (4 oz) button mushrooms
salt and pepper
5 ml (1 level tsp) dried mixed herbs
15 ml (1 level tbsp) cornflour
a little extra wine or stock
chopped parsley to garnish

1 Place the chopped bacon in a large casserole and microwave on HIGH for 2–3 minutes.
2 Add the remaining ingredients, except the cornflour, extra wine or stock and parsley, and mix together.
3 Cover and microwave on HIGH for about 5 minutes or until boiling. Reduce to LOW and cook for a further 40–50 minutes, or until the meat is tender. Stir during cooking.
4 Blend the cornflour with a little extra wine or stock and stir into the casserole.
5 Re-cover and microwave on HIGH to return to the boil and cook for 2–3 minutes, stirring after 2 minutes. If necessary, add a little extra wine or stock at this stage.
6 Garnish with chopped parsley before serving with fluffy boiled rice.

SERVES 4–5

ILLUSTRATED ON PAGE 88

450 g (1 lb) lean minced beef
1 large onion, finely chopped
15 ml (1 level tbsp) chilli
**　powder**
salt and pepper
397-g (14-oz) can tomatoes,
**　chopped**
439-g (15½-oz) can red kidney
**　beans, drained**

Chilli con Carne

1 Crumble the minced beef into a large casserole. Add the onion and microwave on HIGH for about 5 minutes or until the meat is no longer pink. Break up the mince with a fork after 2 minutes.
2 Add chilli powder, salt, pepper and tomatoes with their juice.
3 Cover and microwave on HIGH for about 10 minutes, stirring during cooking.
4 Add the drained kidney beans, re-cover and microwave on HIGH for 5–10 minutes or until heated through.
5 Leave to stand for 5 minutes before serving with fluffy boiled rice or crusty French bread and a green side salad.

SERVES 4

ILLUSTRATED ON PAGE 88

450 g (1 lb) lean minced beef
25 g (1 oz) fresh breadcrumbs
15 ml (1 level tbsp) finely
**　chopped onion**
25 g (1 oz) finely chopped
**　green pepper**
25 g (1 oz) grated Parmesan
salt and pepper
1 egg, beaten

Sauce
425-g (15-oz) can tomato juice
5 ml (1 level tsp) chopped
**　parsley**
salt and pepper

Italian Meatballs

1 Mix together the minced beef, breadcrumbs, onion, green pepper, cheese and seasoning. Bind together with the beaten egg.
2 With wet hands, shape the mixture into 20 small meatballs and place them in a large casserole.
3 Cover and microwave on HIGH for 5–7 minutes, turning the meatballs after 3 minutes.
4 Combine the sauce ingredients, and pour over the meatballs.
5 Cover and microwave on HIGH for 8–10 minutes, or until the meatballs are cooked. Stir gently after every 4 minutes.
6 Serve over cooked spaghetti.

SERVES 4

15 ml (1 tbsp) cooking oil
1 large onion, skinned and
**　finely chopped**
100 g (4 oz) streaky bacon,
**　rinded and chopped**
450 g (1 lb) minced beef or
**　lamb**
397-g (14-oz) can tomatoes in
**　tomato juice**
100 g (4 oz) sliced mushrooms
15 ml (1 tbsp) Worcestershire
**　sauce**
30 ml (2 tbsp) tomato purée
5 ml (1 tsp) mixed herbs
pinch nutmeg
salt and freshly ground pepper

Basic Meat Sauce

1 Heat the oil in a large bowl on HIGH for 30–60 seconds.
2 Stir in the onion and bacon, cover and cook on HIGH for 2–3 minutes or until the onion is soft.
3 Break up the meat and stir in. Cover and cook on HIGH for 2–3 minutes or until meat is no longer pink. Drain off excess fat.
4 Chop the tomatoes and add them, their juice, and the remaining ingredients to the meat mixture.
5 Cover and cook on HIGH for a further 15–20 minutes or until cooked, stirring after 10 minutes, if there is no turntable.

Serving Suggestions
1 Over cooked rice or pasta, sprinkled with Parmesan.
2 As a base for Shepherds Pie—top with hot cooked mashed potato and brown under a preheated conventional grill.
3 As a sauce with pasta or rice, mix together 10 ml (2 level tsp) cornflour with 150 ml (¼ pint) red wine or stock until smooth. Stir in at the end of step 3. Bring to the boil and cook until thickened, stirring once or twice.

Poultry

Microwave ovens do not achieve the same results when cooking poultry as do conventional ovens, but if you follow these guidelines the end product will be perfectly satisfactory.

1 Invest in a non-metal microwave meat thermometer to take the guesswork out of roasting times. Insert it into the thickest part of the thigh. The correct internal temperature should be at least 82–85°C (180–185°F). Temperature will rise by about 5–7°C (10–15°F) during standing time.
2 Improve browning by microwaving in a covered glass casserole or pierced roasting bag (fastened with an elastic band).
3 Brush chicken with soy sauce, melted butter and paprika, or yeast extract diluted with a little hot water to give it colour.
4 Poultry must be completely defrosted before cooking. You can defrost conventionally or in a microwave oven (see page 62), but at present we would recommend thawing in the conventional way if you have time. After defrosting in the microwave oven, birds should still be icy in the centre. To stop the cooking process on the outside but complete defrosting, immerse in cold water.
5 Shield narrow wing tips and bone ends with foil to prevent overcooking.
6 Start cooking whole birds breast side down, and turn after half the cooking time. Larger birds, such as turkeys, are turned over three or four times during cooking.
7 Whole birds should be well trussed to hold wings and legs close to the body, to ensure even cooking.
8 Place poultry on a special microwave roasting rack or upturned saucer to raise it out of its juices during cooking.
9 Small birds benefit from being placed in pierced roasting bags to facilitate browning.
10 Place poultry under a preheated grill or in a conventional oven after cooking by microwaves to produce the traditional crisp brown skin.
11 Leave poultry to stand covered with a tent of foil, shiny side in, for at least 15 minutes after removing from the oven.
12 Increase the cooking time for stuffed poultry by an extra minute per 450 g (1 lb).
13 Cook poultry joints skin side up, placing the thicker parts towards the outside of the dish.

POULTRY COOKING GUIDE

The times given in this chart must only be used as a guide, since there are many variables involved. Follow the oven manufacturer's specific instructions and guidelines for individual models.

Poultry	Approximate Time per 450 g (1 lb) on HIGH	Further Instructions
Whole chicken	6–8 minutes	Turn over breast side up after half the cooking time. Stand, covered in foil, for 10–15 minutes.
Whole duck	7–9 minutes	Turn over breast side up after half the cooking time. Stand, covered in foil, for 10–15 minutes.
Whole turkey	6–7 minutes	Turn over three to four times during cooking. Stand, covered in foil, for 10–15 minutes.
Chicken portions	6–7 minutes	Rearrange during cooking. Stand for 5–10 minutes.

Chicken Breasts Cordon Bleu

4 chicken breasts, skinned and boned
40 g (1½ oz) butter
salt and pepper
4 thin slices boiled ham
4 thin slices Mozzarella cheese
grated Parmesan cheese
paprika

1 Place the chicken breasts between pieces of greaseproof paper or cling film and pound to flatten.

2 Put the butter in a shallow square dish large enough to hold the chicken breasts in a single layer and microwave on HIGH for 30–60 seconds until melted.

3 Add the chicken breasts, turning to coat in the melted butter.

4 Cover and cook on HIGH for 15–20 minutes or until tender. Turn the dish after 10 minutes if the oven does not have a turntable.

5 Drain the chicken and reserve its juices.

6 Season the chicken breasts with salt and pepper.

7 Top each with a slice of ham and then a slice of cheese, brush with reserved juices and sprinkle with Parmesan and paprika.

8 Cover and microwave on HIGH for about 3 minutes or until the cheese just melts.

SERVES 4

Chicken Veronique

50 g (2 oz) butter or margarine
50 g (2 oz) flour
300 ml (½ pint) chicken stock
300 ml (½ pint) dry white wine
or cider
450 g (1 lb) cooked chicken or
turkey meat, cut into 5-cm
(2-inch) pieces
150 ml (¼ pint) single cream
100 g (4 oz) seedless green
grapes
salt and pepper

1 Melt the butter or margarine in a large glass bowl on HIGH for about 30 seconds.
2 Blend in the flour, stock and wine or cider.
3 Microwave on HIGH for 3–5 minutes or until the sauce has thickened, stirring once or twice to prevent lumps.
4 Stir in the cooked chicken meat, cream, grapes and seasoning.
5 Turn into a suitable serving dish.
6 Cover with cling film and microwave on LOW for 4–5 minutes or until heated through. DO NOT ALLOW TO BOIL otherwise the sauce may curdle due to the cream content.
7 Leave to stand for 5 minutes before serving on a bed of cooked savoury or saffron rice.

SERVES 4

Chicken or Turkey Curry

15 g (½ oz) butter or margarine
1 medium onion, finely
chopped
30 ml (2 level tbsp) curry
powder
15 ml (1 level tbsp) flour
600 ml (1 pint) chicken stock
5 ml (1 tsp) Worcestershire
sauce
15 ml (1 level tbsp) tomato
purée
15 ml (1 tbsp) lemon juice
30 ml (2 tbsp) mango chutney
50 g (2 oz) sultanas
1 dessert apple, peeled, cored
and chopped
350–450 g (12 oz–1 lb) cooked
chicken or turkey meat,
cubed
salt and pepper

1 Place the butter or margarine and chopped onion in a casserole. Cover and microwave on HIGH for 3–4 minutes or until the onion is soft.
2 Stir in the curry powder and flour and gradually blend in the stock.
3 Re-cover and microwave on HIGH for about 4 minutes, or until the sauce has thickened. Stir the sauce after every minute.
4 Stir in the Worcestershire sauce, tomato purée, lemon juice, chutney, sultanas and apple.
5 Re-cover and microwave on LOW for about 10 minutes.
6 Add the chicken or turkey meat and seasoning, mixing well.
7 Re-cover and microwave on HIGH for 3–5 minutes, or until heated through.
8 Leave to stand, covered, for 5 minutes before serving with boiled rice.

SERVES 4

Desserts

Most desserts are amazingly successful when cooked in a microwave oven. Suet pastry tastes superb, steamed puddings take minutes instead of hours and dried fruits do not need overnight soaking. Double crust pies, however, need the dry heat of a conventional oven to produce good results. Remember to pierce the skins of whole fruit, such as plums, before cooking to prevent bursting and allow time for desserts to continue to cook by conduction after removal from the oven.

Baked Egg Custard

400 ml (¾ pint) milk
3 eggs, lightly beaten
30 ml (2 level tbsp) caster sugar
grated nutmeg (optional)

1 Place the milk in a glass measuring jug and microwave on HIGH for 1½ minutes or until warm.
2 Add the beaten eggs and sugar and strain into a 900-ml (1½-pint) round ovenproof glass soufflé dish. Sprinkle the nutmeg on top.
3 Cover with cling film and place the dish in a larger dish with a capacity of about 1.75 litres (3 pints). Pour in enough boiling water to come half way up the sides of the dish.
4 Microwave on LOW for 12–18 minutes, or until lightly set. Rotate the dish every 3 minutes during cooking if using an oven without a turntable. Check the set of the custard after 12 minutes.
5 Leave to stand for 5 minutes, remove the soufflé dish from the water, uncover and allow to cool.
6 Refrigerate before serving.

SERVES 3–4

Variations Crème Caramel—Place 45 ml (3 tbsp) sugar and 45 ml (3 tbsp) water in a heatproof jug and microwave on HIGH for 5–6 minutes or until caramelised. Watch carefully once it starts to colour as it will then brown very quickly. Swirl the caramel around a 900-ml (1½-pint) dish, and allow to set while preparing the custard. Pour the custard gently over the set caramel and cook as above. Turn into a serving dish when set and chilled.

Semolina or Ground Rice Pudding

568 ml (1 pint) milk
60 ml (4 level tbsp) semolina or
   ground rice
30 ml (2 level tbsp) caster sugar

1 Place the milk, semolina or ground rice and sugar into a 2-litre (3½-pint) glass bowl.
2 Microwave on HIGH for 5–6 minutes or until the milk boils. Stir.
3 Cover and microwave on HIGH to return to the boil and immediately reduce to LOW and cook for 10–15 minutes until cooked. Stir every 5 minutes.
4 Leave to stand, covered, for 5 minutes and stir before serving.

SERVES 2–3

Creamy Rice Pudding

225 ml (8 fl oz) full cream
    evaporated milk
350 ml (12 fl oz) water
50 g (2 oz) short grain rice
25 g (1 oz) caster sugar

1 Mix the milk and water together.
2 Place, with the rice and sugar, in a buttered 2.75-litre (5-pint) glass bowl. Stir to mix and cover with cling film.
3 Microwave on HIGH for 5–6 minutes or until the liquid is boiling.
4 Immediately reduce to LOW and cook for 35–40 minutes, or until starting to thicken. Stir with a fork to break down any lumps of rice after every 15 minutes and at the end of the cooking time.
5 Leave to stand for 5 minutes to thicken further before serving.

SERVES 3–4

Variations Add 50 g (2 oz) sultanas or raisins to the ingredients and proceed as above. After cooking in the microwave oven, turn the rice into a shallow ovenproof dish and sprinkle with demerara sugar. Place under a preheated conventional grill until sugar has caramelised.

ILLUSTRATED ON PAGE 36

Jam-Capped Suet Pudding

100 g (4 oz) self raising flour
pinch of salt
50 g (2 oz) caster sugar
50 g (2 oz) shredded suet
1 egg, beaten
45 ml (3 tbsp) milk
30 ml (2 tbsp) jam

1 Sieve the flour and salt into a bowl. Add the caster sugar and suet and mix together with the beaten egg and sufficient milk to bind.
2 Place the jam in the base of a greased 600-ml (1-pint) pudding basin, place the mixture on top and level the surface.
3 Microwave on LOW for 6–9 minutes or until the pudding is cooked.
4 Leave to stand for 5 minutes before turning out on to a heated serving dish. Serve with custard sauce (see page 102).

SERVES 4

Variations Replace the jam with stewed fruit, marmalade, canned pie filling or canned fruit.

ILLUSTRATED ON PAGE 36

Stuffed Baked Apples

4 medium cooking apples,
    cored
brown sugar
currants, raisins, sultanas, dates
    or mincemeat

1 Slit the skin round the centre of the apples and place in individual dishes or a suitable serving dish.
2 Fill the centres of the apples with brown sugar and a choice of filling.
3 Cover loosely with buttered greaseproof paper.
4 Microwave on HIGH for $5\frac{1}{2}$–$7\frac{1}{2}$ minutes, or until the fruit is just cooked, but still holds its shape.
5 Leave to stand, covered, for a few minutes before serving.

SERVES 4

Note Cook one apple on HIGH for $2\frac{1}{2}$–3 minutes. Cook two apples on HIGH for $3\frac{1}{2}$–$4\frac{1}{2}$ minutes.

Syrup Sponge Pudding

50 g (2 oz) soft tub margarine
50 g (2 oz) caster sugar
1 egg, beaten
100 g (4 oz) self raising flour
45–60 ml (3–4 tbsp) milk
about 30 ml (2 tbsp) golden
  syrup

1 Beat together the margarine, sugar, egg and flour until smooth. Add the milk gradually to give a soft dropping consistency.
2 Spoon the golden syrup into the bottom of a greased 600-ml (1-pint) pudding basin. Put the sponge mixture on top and level the surface.
3 Microwave on LOW for 7–9 minutes or until the top of the sponge mixture is only slightly moist, and a wooden cocktail stick, inserted in the centre, comes out clean.
4 Leave to stand for 5 minutes before turning out on to a heated serving dish.

SERVES 3–4

Variations Essex pudding—Spread jam over the sides and base of the greased pudding basin. Omit the golden syrup and proceed as above.

Apricot sponge pudding—Drain a 411-g (14½-oz) can of apricot halves and arrange them in the base of the greased pudding basin. Omit the golden syrup and proceed as above.

Grapefruit Wellington

2 grapefruit, cut in half
60 ml (4 tbsp) sherry or kirsch
30 ml (2 tbsp) brown sugar
2 maraschino cherries, cut in
  half

1 Loosen the segments of each grapefruit half with a serrated or grapefruit knife.
2 Pour 15 ml (1 tbsp) sherry or kirsch over each half and sprinkle with brown sugar.
3 Place in individual serving dishes.
4 Arrange the serving dishes in a circle in the oven and microwave on HIGH for about 2 minutes.
5 Decorate with the halved cherries before serving.

SERVES 4

Dried Fruit Compote

350 g (12 oz) dried prunes, figs
  or apricots
400 ml (15 fl oz) water
25 g (1 oz) brown sugar
pinch of ground cinnamon
pinch of mixed spice
15 ml (1 tbsp) brandy

1 Place the dried fruit and water in a suitable dish and cover with cling film.
2 Microwave on HIGH for about 5 minutes.
3 Stir in the remaining ingredients and re-cover.
4 Microwave on HIGH for about 7 minutes.
5 Leave to stand, covered, for about 30 minutes to plump the fruit.
6 Cool and refrigerate before serving.

SERVES 4

Cakes

When baking cakes in a microwave oven, only half-fill your cooking container and leave to stand for 10 minutes before turning out.

Basic Victoria Sandwich Cake

175 g (6 oz) self raising flour
175 g (6 oz) soft tub margarine
175 g (6 oz) caster sugar
3 eggs
30–45 ml (2–3 tbsp) milk

1 Grease a round 19 cm diameter × 10 cm deep ($7\frac{1}{2}$ inches diameter × 4 inches deep) glass soufflé dish and base line with greased greaseproof paper.
2 Mix together the flour, margarine, sugar, eggs and 30 ml (2 tbsp) of the milk in a mixing bowl. Beat until smooth. If necessary, add a further 15 ml (1 tbsp) milk to give a soft dropping consistency.
3 Place the mixture into the prepared dish and microwave on HIGH for $5\frac{1}{2}$–$7\frac{1}{2}$ minutes or until cooked in the centre when a wooden cocktail stick inserted into the centre comes out clean. If oven has no turntable, place the cake on an upturned plate and rotate every 2 minutes during cooking.
4 Stand for 5–10 minutes before turning on to a wire rack.
5 When completely cold, split in half and fill with jam and cream or buttercream. Dust the top of the cake with sieved icing sugar.

Variations Orange or lemon sandwich cake—Replace some of the milk with the juice of 1 orange or 1 lemon and the grated rind and proceed as above. When cold, split and fill with orange or lemon flavoured buttercream.

Moist Chocolate Sandwich Cake

ILLUSTRATED ON PAGE 35

100 g (4 oz) golden syrup
100 g (4 oz) soft dark brown sugar
100 g (4 oz) butter or margarine
175 g (6 oz) self raising flour
50 g (2 oz) cocoa
1 egg, beaten
150 ml ($\frac{1}{4}$ pint) single cream or milk

Topping
100 g (4 oz) plain chocolate or cake covering
100 ml (4 fl oz) double cream, whipped
flaked almonds, halved walnuts or chocolate curls

1 Cut a strip of greaseproof paper to line the base and each end of a 23-cm (9-inch) loaf dish.
2 Place syrup, brown sugar and butter or margarine in a large ovenproof bowl and microwave on HIGH for about 2 minutes or until ingredients are melted. Stir.
3 Add sieved flour and cocoa, mixing well together.
4 Beat in egg and then stir in the cream or milk.
5 Place the mixture in the prepared dish and cook for about 5 minutes, on HIGH or until cooked in the centre when tested. Rotate the container after every 2 minutes if the oven does not have a turntable.
6 Leave cake to stand 5 minutes before turning out to cool.
7 When completely cold, break the chocolate or cake covering into small pieces, place in a small bowl and microwave on HIGH for about 1 minute to melt, stirring after 30 seconds.
8 Spread the melted chocolate over the top of the cake, allowing it to dribble over the edges and sides. Leave to set.
9 Decorate the top with piped cream and either flaked almonds, halved walnuts or chocolate curls.

MAKES ONE 23-cm (9-inch) LOAF-SHAPED CAKE

ILLUSTRATED ON PAGE 35

Rich Fruit Cake

2 eggs
100 g (4 oz) soft dark brown
    sugar
30 ml (2 tbsp) black treacle
60 ml (4 tbsp) oil
175 g (6 oz) self raising flour
2.5 ml ($\frac{1}{2}$ tsp) baking powder
5 ml (1 tsp) mixed spice
2.5 ml ($\frac{1}{2}$ tsp) salt
100 ml (4 fl oz) milk
750 g (1$\frac{1}{2}$ lb) mixed dried fruit
50 g (2 oz) glacé cherries,
    quartered
100 g (4 oz) mixed chopped
    nuts
brandy

Topping
apricot jam
walnut halves
glacé cherries, halved

1 Base-line a 20-cm (8-inch) round ovenproof soufflé dish.
2 Beat together the eggs, sugar, treacle and oil in a large mixing bowl.
3 Sieve the dry ingredients, and stir in alternately with the milk. Stir in fruit and nuts.
4 Spoon the mixture into the prepared dish. Level the top.
5 Microwave on LOW for 30–40 minutes, or until cooked when tested, in the centre. Rotate the dish every 10 minutes, if the oven does not have a turntable.
6 Leave in the dish for at least 30 minutes, before turning out onto a cooling rack.
7 When cold, skewer with brandy, and store, wrapped in grease-proof paper and foil to mature for about one week.
8 To decorate, spread a little warmed apricot jam over the cake and arrange walnut and cherry halves on top.

MAKES ONE 20-cm (8-inch) CAKE

ILLUSTRATED ON PAGE 35

Lemon and Hazelnut Cake

100 g (4 oz) butter or
    margarine
100 g (4 oz) caster sugar
grated rind of lemon
2 eggs
75 g (3 oz) self raising flour
25 g (1 oz) ground hazelnuts
30 ml (2 tbsp) warm water

Topping
juice of 1 lemon
30 ml (2 tbsp) caster sugar
30 ml (2 tbsp) ground
    hazelnuts

Filling
300 ml ($\frac{1}{2}$ pint) whipping
    cream, whipped
fresh raspberries or
    strawberries

1 Cream the fat and sugar till light and fluffy.
2 Add the grated lemon rind and beat in the eggs gradually.
3 Fold in the flour, hazelnuts and water.
4 Turn the mixture into a 21.5-cm (8$\frac{1}{2}$-in) ovenproof glass savarin or a base-lined 18-cm (7-inch) soufflé dish. Smooth the top.
5 Microwave on HIGH for approximately 4–5 minutes, or until cooked, when tested, in the centre. Rotate the dish after 2 minutes if the oven does not have a turntable.
6 Leave to stand for 5–10 minutes, before turning out onto a cooling rack.
7 Mix together the lemon juice and caster sugar. Pour this over the top of the cake while still warm and sprinkle with ground hazelnuts.
8 When completely cold, place on a plate and fill with whipped cream and fresh fruit.

MAKES ONE 20-cm (8-inch) CAKE

Bread

Bread baked in a microwave oven does not brown nor produce a crisp crust. If this bothers you, place under a preheated grill for a few minutes before serving.

Wholewheat Loaf

5 ml (1 level tsp) caster sugar
5 ml (1 level tsp) dried yeast
300 ml (½ pint) water
450 g (1 lb) wholewheat flour
2.5 ml (½ level tsp) salt
15 g (½ oz) butter or margarine

1 Mix the sugar and dried yeast with 100 ml (4 fl oz) of the water at a temperature of 43°C (110°F). Leave in a warm place for about 10 minutes until frothy.

2 Place the flour and salt in a mixing bowl and microwave on HIGH for about 30 seconds or until warm.

3 Rub in the butter or margarine and mix to a dough with the yeast liquid and the remaining water at 43°C (110°F). Depending on the flour used, it may be necessary to add a further 15–30 ml (1–2 tbsp) water if the dough is too dry.

4 Knead the dough until smooth in texture and no longer sticky.

5 Shape and place in a suitable greased container.

6 Cover with a polythene bag or cling film and leave in a warm place until doubled in size.

7 Remove cover and microwave either on HIGH for 6 minutes, or on LOW for 12 minutes, until cooked through, rotating the dish every 2 minutes if the oven has no turntable.

8 Turn out of the container and brown under a preheated conventional grill for a few minutes, if liked.

MAKES ONE 450-g (1-lb) LOAF

All-Bran Tea Bread

100 g (4 oz) All-Bran
75 g (3 oz) soft dark brown sugar
225 g (8 oz) mixed dried fruit
50 g (2 oz) nuts, chopped
250 ml (½ pint) milk
100 g (4 oz) self raising flour

1 Grease a 20 × 12.5 × 6-cm (8 × 5 × 2½-inch) loaf-shaped dish and base line with greased greaseproof paper.

2 Place the All-Bran, sugar, fruit and nuts in a bowl. Pour over the milk and leave to soak for 1½–2 hours.

3 Stir in the flour, mixing well.

4 Turn the mixture into the prepared dish. Press down firmly and level the surface.

5 Place on an upturned plate if the oven has no turntable.

6 Microwave on LOW for 14–16 minutes, or until the centre is cooked, when a wooden cocktail stick inserted into the centre comes out clean. Rotate the dish on the upturned plate every 2–3 minutes.

7 Leave to stand for 5 minutes before turning out to cool.

8 When cold, wrap and store for 1–2 days before serving sliced and buttered.

MAKES ONE 20 × 12.5-cm (8 × 5-inch) LOAF

Sauces

Most sauces may be made in advance, in the same jug in which you want to serve them, and reheated as required—no more burnt saucepans to wash up! Do choose a dish large enough to prevent spills, especially with milk-based sauces, and stir them once or twice during cooking.

Basic White Sauce

Pouring sauce
25 g (1 oz) soft tub margarine
25 g (1 oz) flour
300 ml ($\frac{1}{2}$ pint) milk
salt and pepper

Coating sauce
50 g (2 oz) soft tub margarine
50 g (2 oz) flour
300 ml ($\frac{1}{2}$ pint) milk
salt and pepper

1 Combine all the ingredients in a glass measuring jug, blending well together.
2 Microwave on HIGH for $3\frac{1}{2}$–$4\frac{1}{2}$ minutes or until the sauce has boiled and thickened, stirring after every minute.

Variations The following ingredients may be added to the sauce for the final 2 minutes cooking time.
Cheese sauce Add 50–75 g (2–3 oz) grated cheese.
Mushroom sauce Add 75 g (3 oz) sliced, lightly cooked or canned mushrooms.
Parsley sauce Add 15 ml (1 tbsp) chopped parsley.
Caper sauce Add 15–30 ml (1–2 tbsp) chopped capers.
Onion sauce Add 100 g (4 oz) chopped cooked onion.
Egg sauce Add 1 finely chopped hard-boiled egg.

Apple Sauce

450 g (1 lb) cooking apples,
   peeled, cored and sliced
15 ml (1 tbsp) water
15 g ($\frac{1}{2}$ oz) butter
lemon juice
sugar to taste

ILLUSTRATED ON PAGE 36

1 Place ingredients in a suitable dish and cover with cling film.
2 Microwave on HIGH for 6–8 minutes until apples are soft.
3 Beat well until smooth, or sieve or liquidise.
4 Serve with pork, roast duck or use as required.

MAKES ABOUT 300 ml ($\frac{1}{2}$ pint)

Custard Sauce

15–30 ml (1–2 tbsp) sugar
30 ml (2 level tbsp) or 600-ml
   (1-pint) packet custard
   powder
568 ml (1 pint) milk

1 Blend the sugar and custard powder, with a little of the measured milk, in a glass measuring jug or bowl.
2 Stir in the rest of the milk.
3 Microwave on HIGH for 3–4 minutes or until thickened, stirring after every 2 minutes. Stir well and serve.

Jam or Marmalade Sauce

100 g (4 oz) jam or marmalade
2.5 ml ($\frac{1}{2}$ level tsp) arrowroot or
   cornflour
few drops of lemon juice

1 Place the jam or marmalade and 150 ml ($\frac{1}{4}$ pint) water in a suitable bowl and microwave on HIGH for 2 minutes.
2 Blend the arrowroot or cornflour with the 30 ml (2 tbsp) water until smooth and stir into the heated mixture.
3 Microwave on HIGH for 1–2 minutes or until boiling, stirring after 1 minute.
4 Add lemon juice to taste, and sieve if preferred before serving.

INDEX